Money Circle

What choice are you willing to make today to create a
different future right away?

Nilofer Safdar

DEDICATION

This book is dedicated to YOU, the reader, the listener of my telesummits and teleseries, and to all the amazing individuals all over the world who are on a quest, a journey of self-discovery.

This is a reminder about your own Greatness, the infinite capacities and abilities you have and the infinite possibilities that are available to you.

I thank you for being a part of my own journey and all that you have contributed to me.

I honor you and the infinite potential within you!

TABLE OF CONTENTS

FOREWORD

I met Nilofer online through her *Illusion to Illumination* summit. Since then I am in awe with her ease of creation and childlike joy. For Nilofer even sky is not the limit. She dreams big, bigger and even bigger as she moves through her life sweeping the bystanders along with her in her adventure. She has a unique style of facilitation through giggles that gently cuts through the limitations without even a sliver of intensity exposing the truth behind them. I am so proud to have her as my laughing partner and so honored to write the foreword for her book, *The Money Circle*. How does it get any better than this?®

This book is a collection of Nilofer's facilitation through money circles and surely allows the reader to experience the immense changes the circle created for the participants. Throughout the book we can see how Nilofer refuses to buy into the illusion of limitation. By doing so, she creates the space for the participants to see new possibilities. One could easily get offended when the facilitator does not validate the story but Nilofer, with her charm, not only cruises through this easily; she also inspires the readers to give up their stories without much resistance.

Even if the reader has a strong tendency to hold on to their stories, the third chapter, *What is your money story?,* will challenge them wittingly and get them out of the illusion before their mind realizes that by the time the reader finishes this book, they will actually start creating their financial reality from their knowing instead of their stories.
There is no doubt that this book will nudge the readers to receive from every molecule of this universe - yes, even from toxic waste! Here is an exercise from chapter 2:

"Now perceive a garbage dump or a toxic waste site. Do you have your barriers up or your barriers down? Push your barriers down and perceive what it feels like to have your barriers down in this place. What if you were not to label it as a toxic waste or garbage dump? Would you perceive it as free-flowing energy? What if it was just free-flowing energy? Could you use this energy? Could this energy be a contribution to your life, your living, your reality, your money flows and your bank accounts?"

Did you experience the shift? This is just a small sample from the ocean of goodies this book offers. Nilofer has dealt with each participant differently by empowering them with the vast number of tools from the chest of Access Consciousness ®.

Money is a serious business in this reality. Yet this book will facilitate the readers into having fun with creating and generating money. Have you ever asked, "How much money would be fun for me?" I am sure before finishing this book; this question will become your mantra as Nilofer has a compelling knack for selling the benefits of asking this question.

Besides having fun, Nilofer will also trick you into claiming your magical capacities. Well, if you don't want to be that magical, don't read this book!

"What energy, space and consciousness can you and your body be to be the magic, the wizardry, the witchcraft and the sorcery you truly be for all eternity? Everything that doesn't allow that, destroy and uncreate it times Godzillion. Right and Wrong, Good and Bad, POD, POC, All 9, Shorts, Boys and Beyonds®"

While this book is set out to demystify the myths around money, the wide range of tools shared in this book can be used in any area of your life to create future possibilities. This book will also facilitate you to be more of you, be present in your life, include your body in the computation of your life, open you up to receiving more and have loads of fun, if you choose. What magic can you be for you?

Infinite gratitude,
Nirmala Raju (Nimi)
Medium, Healer and Facilitator

Feel free to download free *Expanding Your Relationship with Ease* class by subscribing to my newsletter:
www.infinitehealing.co.uk

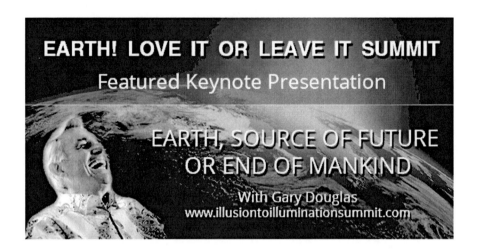

Earth! Love It Or Leave It Summit

What would it be like if we became stewards of Earth rather than continuously taking everything we can from it?

What future could we create if we realized that this is the planet that we will be living on for generations to come?

This can only be a reality on planet Earth if WE, as mankind, make some drastically different choices.
And the truth of it is that those choices are not about protesting against pollution, trying to save the whales, or anything like that.

They are the culmination of the consciousness that you're willing to be and function from, rather than the trauma, drama and misery that we all make more real than us.

Join us at http://www.illusiontoilluminationsummit.com

INTRODUCTION

Most of the tools I share in this book are from Access Consciousness®. I am so grateful for Gary Douglas and Dr. Dain Heer, the founders of Access Consciousness®, for their contribution to creating more consciousness on Planet Earth. My life has completely changed since I have been using the tools of Access Consciousness®. In this book I'd like to share with you some of the tools I have used to completely change my money situation and create a phenomenal business.

My Story

When I was a little girl, money was tight. I remember lying down in bed one night and thinking, "I'm always going to have lots of money, so I never have to struggle for anything again."

After graduating I created my own business and created an ease with money. I had read somewhere that money was the easiest thing to demonstrate, and I had created that in my life. That was a magical time in my life. I was travelling all over India promoting my business having lots of fun. Then I created a trip to Germany. What was magical about that trip was that I created money for it seemingly out of thin air. My suppliers gave me credit when they had never done so before. My clients paid me in advance for a huge order. I was in Germany for 40 days, alone for the first time in my life. It was so much fun.

After I got married, I moved to Saudi Arabia. Once again I stepped into a contraction with money. I bought into the lie that my husband was the source of my abundance. So I would use tools and techniques every day to improve his financial reality, so that my financial reality would improve. Nothing seemed to work. Until one day I had this huge epiphany!

I am the creator source of *MY* reality.

By buying into the lie that my husband was the source of my abundance, I had stopped creating my reality. I was living his reality. I could not fix or change his reality. I could only create and change my reality. That was the day everything shifted for me.

I started creating my reality again. Within a month, my husband got a promotion and a pay hike at his job. A few months later, I found a job in a school working as a teacher. I had abundance again.

We moved to Abu Dhabi in 2005. I started doing what I loved to do. I started healing people and facilitating people. I created money to pay for my workshops, some of which included travel to USA and Russia.

In 2012 I found Access Consciousness®. I attended the core classes: Bars, Foundation and Level One. Just then I said, "I'm going to use the tools to expand my business and create more money in my life." I started working with the tools in September. By January I had made more money than I had ever made in my life. It was phenomenal!

Since then I am aware just how much I am actually creating my reality. Whatever I desire, I know I can create. It is as simple as that.

Last year I facilitated a teleseries, which I titled *Money Circle*.

This book is created from that teleseries. There are 9 chapters. Each chapter has at least one tool you can play with for a suggested duration of one week's time. People have had amazing things show up during the 9 weeks. Of course, you are invited to use the tools for more than a week. Whatever is light for you. Whatever will create more for you. Allow your awareness to guide you.

This book is full of tools that you can use to create whatever you desire. The caveat is that you have to use the tools.

Below is a comment someone made during the teleseries and my response to it, which illustrates the tools work if you work the tools.

Caller: "Wow, I can see Access is really working for you. What an inspiration you are!"

Nilofer: Access Consciousness® is working for me because I work the tools of Access Consciousness®. When I attended one of my first Access classes, *Foundation Level 1*, I heard the facilitator talking about this woman. The facilitator said, "Oh, I heard that she fell and she sprained her ankle. She's been in a lot of pain for the last 2 or 3 weeks and she did not choose to reach out to me or reach out to somebody else to have them facilitate her."

When I heard her say that, I felt, "wow, that's so true." How often do we go into our own misery, and we just want to wallow in that misery. We don't want to reach out to somebody and have them facilitate us. So I had a friend who attended *Foundation Level 1* class with me. I said to her, "Let's make a demand of ourselves and will you support me in this?" I asked her, "Every time I am in my stuff, can I pick up the phone and call you, and will you facilitate me out of that contraction?" She said, "Yes." She asked me to do the same. We became buddies. Every time we would go into whatever stuff was going on in our lives, we reached out and asked each other to facilitate us out of that stuff.

That's all there is. I made a demand that day that no matter what it takes, I'm not going to wallow in anything for a long period of time. I am going to get out of it. I am either going to reach out to her and work with her, or I am finding that I will just use the tools even more. The first thing that I did even then was to use the tools to shift things for me. Only when I felt totally overwhelmed and required some more help, would I actually call her.

Sometimes even she could not facilitate me. Then I would think about "Who can I get in touch with? Who can facilitate me?" Just ask who can be a contribution here, and they are a contribution. Ever since I have used the tools in the last couple of years, I have had such major Aha! moments with the tools. I changed things going on in my body. I changed things going on in my relationship.

By using simple tools like saying "What else is possible?®" and just saying it over and over again, day and night, for the next 2 days or for the next 15 days; I absolutely know that things shift for me. I go to that place of demand that "I don't care what it takes but this thing has to change for me. I am not willing to settle for anything less than that." I am willing to do whatever it takes. I am willing to use the tools and to abuse the tools, literally. I will take a tool and use it till the kingdom comes. I will say "What else is possible?®" one million times if that is what it takes to shift things for me. Are you willing to do that? If you are willing to do that, you can change anything and everything in your life.

I changed my money situation. I have expanded my business beyond what I ever thought was possible. I changed things going on in my body. I changed things going on in my relationship, because I was not willing to settle for anything less than that. Are you willing to settle for anything less than that? Use the tools. You have all the tools available to you, so just use them. Access will work for you if you work Access in your life.

There are some things which come up again and again. I have left them as so. Reading about the same tool in different situations will gift you new awarenesses.

What people said about the Money Circle Series

"Thank you for this awesome series. What a gift of awesome contribution to me it is! Income increased by at least $3,000 per month so far! And gifted $1,500." How does it get any better than that?® What else is possible?® Yay! Woo-hoo! And what would it take for more of that to show up? What would it take for me to out-create that 1,000-fold today?"

"This has been wonderful! Things are changing dramatically for me. Just found out that I will be receiving $4,500 from the government that I definitely wasn't expecting! How does it get any better than that?® What else is possible?®"

"I love where my money energy is going. After a month on these clearing loops and doing the work on a minimal basis, I had $6,000 more and $3,000 was a gift from someone. How does it get any better than this?®"

"I was full of energy and managed to get rid of some clutter that was surrounding me for a while."

"Hi Nilofer, just wanted to say that the calls so far have all been an awesome contribution, thank you, thank you! What would it take to extend the series to 100 calls?!?!"

AN AFTERTHOUGHT

DO YOU HAVE A CEILING TO THE MONEY YOU CAN HAVE?

"Ask and you shall receive! It is never a money problem."
~ Gary Douglas

This chapter is a bonus, almost an afterthought. I had compiled this book a few months ago. And it just would not move. The different steps in moving it forward were going at a snails pace. My beautiful friend, Nila, kept asking me about this book. I just kind of kept ignoring it.

So one day I reached out to her and asked if she would facilitate me on this.

Here is what she said, "Have you asked the book for contribution and also contribution from the people who are waiting to read it?" Wow!! That totally changed my reality.

The next day I was being interviewed on a telesummit. Guess what it was about?
MONEY.

After the interview, the book spoke to me. It wanted the interview in here.

You know that thing, "You get it when you get it when you get it!!!!"

This was the missing piece in the book.

Interview with Lianne Soller, *Healthy and Wealthy Entrepreneur Summit*

Lianne (L): The title for our talk today is *Do you have a ceiling to the money you can have? And how you can bust it.*

So what do you mean by this title exactly?

Nilofer (N): Have you ever had some of those months when you have more money come in than usual and at the same time you have an unexpected expense show up, like something goes kaput in your house or maybe your car or you fall sick and you have an unexpected hospital bill? Have you ever had that happen?

L: Definitely, yes.

N: Yes. So that is exactly what I am talking about. You are familiar with the concept of a thermostat, right? When we set the temperature of a thermostat to a particular figure, if the temperature goes above it, the thermostat brings it back to that temperature. If it goes below it, it will bring it back to the set temperature. In the same way, we have a money ceiling. What I mean by that is this is the amount of money that you can tolerate.

It is literally the amount of money that you can tolerate to receive, the amount of money that you can tolerate to have. So what happens is that if you receive more money than this, guess what you have to do? You have to create an unexpected expense so that the money goes away towards that. Or if you create less than that, that is good news, as you will most likely end up creating more money, which will match your ceiling.

This is really very interesting to me, because I have always been very fascinated by money. When I was young, when money was not that abundant at home and I would want something, I would tell my mom and she would say "Oh, you know, we do not have money for this. We do not have money for that."

I remember lying down in bed one night thinking, "I am never ever going to be in this place where I do not have money to do something that I want to do. So I am always going to have more money than that." Now when I look back at whatever has been happening in my life, I have always managed to create that money. When I think about those times, I think that if I can lie down in my bed, think something and actually create that; then is it possible that something else than what we are doing is actually governing the amount of money that we are willing to have.

That started out my whole enquiry.

What was fascinating was that I started trying to make money online about 7 or 8 years ago. It just would not come together for me. I would do a whole lot of things. I would be chasing the next bright, shiny object thinking, "Oh, if I do this then finally I will be able to make money. Or if I do that I will be able to make money."

Then what happened was I touched that moment of magic for me where suddenly I started to make a lot of money. What I realized was that it was not so much what I was doing externally, as in terms of strategies and things like that; it was more of what kind of change I was making in my inner landscape that was creating me being able to receive the money.

That is what I would actually love to talk about with you today. I would love to lead you through a few questions which will allow you to see where your inner landscape is about money and how you can change it. Would you be open to doing that?

L: Yes, for sure. I am really curious to know what my money ceiling is all about. I know that money for me is kind of this taboo thing, where it is like "Oh, do not talk about money." We never talked about money in my household when I was growing up. We never talked about that with my friends. So, I feel there is definitely a block that I would love to work on. And so yes, I am totally open to this.

N: Ok. So here is what I am going to do. I am going to share with you a tool. This tool may sound really, really, very weird to you.

L: Ok.

N: But here is my invitation to you and I love laughing about it. Here is my invitation to you. Use it, and see what change it creates in your life.

You have the saying, "The proof of the pudding is in the taste." So you could look at this pudding, which looks like this ghastly shade of green. Yet, you put it into your mouth and it just is totally orgasmic on your taste buds. This analogy suits the tool I'm sharing with you.

L: Yes

N: We have all heard of Harry Potter and his magic wand. I am going to give you a magic wand today.

L: Yes.

N: So, the tools I am going to use today in our conversation are from this body of work called Access Consciousness®. This particular tool is called, *The Clearing Statement*. The clearing statement is like a magic wand. When I ask you a question, all your blocks and limitations will start to show up energetically. Then I will ask you, "Will you destroy and uncreate it?" So what you are doing is, you are destroying the blocks and limitations. And why do I say uncreate? Uncreate is because at some point, you are the one who has created that block or limitation. So we will uncreate that. And then I will use the clearing statement, which is this bunch of weird words "Right and Wrong, Good and Bad, POD, POC, All 9, Shorts, Boys and Beyonds®" You can just go to this website called www.theclearingstatement.com to find an explanation.

You can just say "All the weird words Nilofer said" and even that will work, you can say "Pod and poc" or you can say "Clearing statement." It will work.

L: Yes.

N: What I would like you to do is rewind a little bit. You started talking about money. Then you said there was this weirdness about money, and money was a taboo subject.

L: Yes

N: Do you remember at that point when you were saying that, could you actually feel in your body that sense of constriction, limitation and everything?

L: Yes, definitely.

N: And you can connect with it right now?

L: Yes

N: The moment you talk about money, all your limitations and everything show up. It is there around you, forming these huge walls around you. No matter how much you try to break through it, you are not able to break through it to expand out to receive more.

L: Okay.

WHAT DOES MONEY MEAN TO YOU?

N: So let me ask you a question. What does money mean to you?

L: Money means freedom. It means happiness. It means success. Yes.

N: Can I be a little intrusive with this?

L: Of course.

N: So when you say freedom, happiness and success is that what you are experiencing in your body right now? Or is it the opposite that you are experiencing?

L: I am experiencing the opposite of those words.

N: Exactly. "This is something I should be having, but I absolutely do not have right now." That is the energy of it.

Everything that brings up, will you destroy and uncreate it please? Right and Wrong, Good and Bad, POD, POC, All 9, Shorts, Boys and Beyonds®

Can you feel that sense of a little bit of relaxation?

L: Yes, I actually can. That is really strange. I was not sure it would work.

N: Yes, yes, absolutely. Like I said, the proof of the pudding lies in the taste. So try it.

L: Yes

N: So let me ask you this once again. So what does money mean to you?

L: Money means joy and love, amazing relationships, time and freedom to travel around the world and experience new things, new cultures and new foods. See the world differently.

N: Now did you notice when you answered me this time, your energy was way more expansive. It was way more of "Yes, I would like to have this."

L: Yes, and I actually was smiling while I was telling it to you.

N: Exactly. So do you see how your energy shifted from the first question and the clearing statement to this?

L: Yes, right.

N: So everything that does not allow you to perceive, know, be and receive money as everything that you just said, will you destroy and uncreate that? Right and Wrong, Good and Bad, POD, POC, All 9, Shorts, Boys and Beyonds®

I am going to ask you one last time the same question. What does money mean to you?

L: Money means travelling around the world, meeting new people, experiencing new places, new things and new cultures, having fun, being really happy, being very successful and having everything that I want in my life.

N: So everything that does not allow you to have all of that, will you destroy and uncreate it please? Right and Wrong, Good and Bad, POD, POC, All 9, Shorts, Boys and Beyonds®

Now let me ask you a different question.

ARE YOU WILLING TO HAVE MONEY?

What is the amount of money that you would like to create in your business this year? And you do not actually have to tell me the amount, but just think that amount.

L: Yes. Okay.

N: So on a scale of zero to ten, how much do you think that you will be able to create it? Where ten means you are absolutely sure you will have it, and zero means you are totally sure that you will not have it.

L: I say, probably six.

N: Let me ask you this. What stops you from creating it?

L: Confidence. And lack of skills and sales, I guess.

N: Let me ask you this. So are you sure that you do not have confidence?

L: No.

N: Because you are putting together a telesummit, my dear. If you did not have confidence, you would not put yourself out there in front of all those people.

L: Yes, that is true.

N: So is that a lie you are telling yourself?

L: It might be. It could be just an excuse.

N: Yes.

All the lies that you are telling yourself that stop you from receiving this money and creating it in your business this year, will you destroy and uncreate it please? Right and Wrong, Good and Bad, POD, POC, All 9, Shorts, Boys and Beyonds®

How many lies are you using to refuse the money you could be choosing?

L: Hmm, probably a lot.

N: Everything that is, will you destroy and uncreate please? Right and Wrong, Good and Bad, POD, POC, All 9, Shorts, Boys and Beyonds®

I would like to point out one thing for you. Do you notice that when I ask you a question, sometimes you do not even have words but you just have this weird energy around you?

L: Yes

N: So this is really non-cognitive. So if you do not get words, it does not really matter. The moment I ask you the question, we are pulling up all those energies which are limiting you.

L: Right.

N: The other thing you said was the lack of skills.

Truth: do you really lack the skills that you require to *receive* that money?

L: No.

N: (laughs) Okay, cool.

L: No, I do not. (laughs)

N: Everything that is, will you destroy and uncreate it please? Right and Wrong, Good and Bad, POD, POC, All 9, Shorts, Boys and Beyonds®

It is literally these things that we believe, these points of view that we have, that are limiting our money flows. It is almost like a person who is working at a job and they go, "Oh, if I just had more qualifications, I would get that promotion and that pay hike." Then he goes on to study an MBA. Then at the end of the MBA, again, he is in the same dead-end job. He is still at that place of no promotion, because he got the qualification and he did not really make the shift inside to be able to receive that promotion.

L: Yes, that makes sense.

N: How many points of view are you using to limit the receiving of money you are choosing?

L: Probably a lot. Yes, I would say, probably a lot of negative points of view for sure.

N: Yes, so everything that is, will you destroy and uncreate it please? Right and Wrong, Good and Bad, POD, POC, All 9, Shorts, Boys and Beyonds®

N: I would like you to think of that figure that I asked you to think about before. (For everyone reading, I invite you to do the same.) What is the amount of money you would like to create and now look at that scale from zero to ten, so what number is it at right now?

L: It is like a 9.5 out of 10.

N: Oh my god, how does it get any better than this? Let me ask you one more question, that one question which will actually push you through to that 10.

Truth: are you willing to have that money?

L: Oh, that is a tough one. I think I want it, but it is like scary to have it. You know?

N: Exactly. Everything that is, will you destroy and uncreate it please? Right and Wrong, Good and Bad, POD, POC, All 9, Shorts, Boys and Beyonds®

COMFORT ZONES WITH MONEY

How many comfort zones are you using to refuse that money you are choosing?

L: A lot. Many, many.

N: Everything that is, will you destroy and uncreate it please? Right and Wrong, Good and Bad, POD, POC, All 9, Shorts, Boys and Beyonds®

Here is something really interesting for you. What if you were to expand that comfort zone? What if you were to expand that zone? Let us not call it comfort anymore. What if you were to expand that zone to actually be able to receive that amount of money?

L: That would be great. (laughs)

N: Yes, and did you notice that you just did it as I was talking to you about it? Could you feel that sense of expansion in your energy?

L: Well, yes. When you asked me how I would feel, I was like, "Oh yes, it would be pretty cool."

N: Everything that does not allow you to perceive, know, be and receive that, will you destroy and uncreate it please? Right and Wrong, Good and

Bad, POD, POC, All 9, Shorts, Boys and Beyonds®

What would it be like to have that amount of money?

L: That would be like—I do not know—just like a relief, you know. Like "Wow, I have this." (laughs) "It is amazing."

N: Yes. And do you notice that now when I ask you that question, you are able to receive that much more easily than before?

L: Yes, definitely. Yes.

N: Everything that does not allow it, will you destroy and uncreate it please? Right and Wrong, Good and Bad, POD, POC, All 9, Shorts, Boys and Beyonds®

L: That is so funny. So I – like it was funny, because when we started this and you asked me if I was open to do it, I was like, "Yes, let us do it. Let us see what happens. Let us see if it works. Let us see if any changes can be made." And when you asked me if I felt any differently, you know, I probably would not have tapped into that unless you asked me the questions. So I really appreciated you allowing me to feel the differences and actually experience it, because I do feel that when I talk about money with people. There is this constriction, almost like I cannot breathe extensively. I feel like my muscles are all clenched up. So you allowed me to let that go, and really stand and just feel the receiving of this money and having this money.

ARE YOUR MONEY LIMITATIONS YOURS?

N: Can I actually add one more piece to that?

L: Yes.

N: Because if I do not add this piece, then there will be something incomplete here. We are all really psychic. So what do I mean by this? What I mean by this is we are really, really, really, very, very, very, very, very aware. 98% of our thoughts, feelings and emotions are actually not ours. We are just aware of stuff from all around us.

L: Yes, okay.

N: And what I mean by all around us, it does not mean just people living in the house with you or maybe in the building, it could mean within an 8 mile to an 8,000 mile radius.

L: That is brilliant.

N: Now here is the thing, how many people do you know who do not have a funky energy around money?

L: Not many people. Not many.

N: Right? It could be like 0.00001%, right?

L: Yes.

N: So today we let go of all this. Then tomorrow you are talking with somebody and you have this funky energy show up again. You may be apt to think, "Hmm, but I just did that session with Nilofer yesterday. So, it did not really go away." So my question is, "Is that funky energy you are aware of yours? Or are you simply aware of the funky energy around money?"

L: Yes, I think you are right. I think most people that I would talk to would also have that funky energy.

N: Yes, absolutely. So what you have to be willing to do is ask a question. You have to ask a question like "Who does this belong to?®"

L: Okay.

N: So when you ask this question, "Who does this belong to?®" and that energy lightens up, what it means it that none of it is yours.

L: Right.

N: So you can just say, "Return it all back to sender with consciousness attached."

L: Oh, I love that.

N: So you are returning it all back to sender and a lot of us feel, "Oh, I do not want to send them back their funky energy." Yet you know, we are saying, "With consciousness attached". So when you attach consciousness then they also have a different possibility available to them.

L: Okay, so you are making them more aware I guess.

N: Yes, if they choose it. Because again, it is this whole conversation of you can lead a horse to the water, but whether he drinks it is his choice.

L: Yes. Yes. That is right.

L: I was thinking I am going to have to prepare questions for you. I mean, I could have prepared many questions, but that was really, really helpful to actually go through this process. I hope that our readers will gain some clarity and are going to start looking into this too, because most, like you said and we talked about, most of us do have blocks around money.

N: Here is the thing; it is not just you who went through this. Everyone who is reading, if you are willing to receive it, you can just receive it. You will actually let go of some of your blocks to receiving money, as well. What you and I have been doing, it is an experiential energy that is available everyone who reads this. (I invite all our readers to read this again and again because every time you read it, you will actually touch a different layer of your blocks and your stuff around money.)

CHAPTER ONE

CAPACITIES WITH MONEY

What capacities do you have for creating money, wealth and abundance that you haven't yet acknowledged?

All of us have these capacities for creating money, wealth and abundance. Look back in your life for times when you asked for something, including money, and it just showed up as if by magic. All of us have some of these stories. All of us have had these occasions when money just showed up as if by magic, as if it was from thin air. These are the times when you were actually tapping into your capacity for creating money.

What capacities for creating money, wealth, abundance, riches and gold do you have that you are not acknowledging that if you were to acknowledge them, would give you more money than God? Everything that doesn't allow you to perceive, know, be and receive money, wealth, abundance, riches and gold will you destroy and uncreate it all? Right and Wrong, Good and Bad, POD, POC, All 9, Shorts, Boys and Beyonds®

If you look back in your life, you will find these instances where you were able to create money as if by magic and where you were able to create things, opportunities, and a whole lot of stuff as if by magic.

MAGIC DIARY

What I would like you to do is to have a little notebook, your little magic diary, which you use to start listing out all these instances in your life where you have created by magic. Every time you find one of those instances, say, "Wow, I created that!" and "What would it take for me to have more of that?" Acknowledge *every* occasion, every time that you created this magic of money, wealth and abundance in your life.

Every time you acknowledge something, you are asking for more of it to show up in your life using the question "What would it take for me to have more of that to show up in my life?"

When I started using this tool, I started getting all these dreams of money, wealth and riches. It was almost like I was tapping into all those times in my existence when I had been able to create all that money and I was claiming, owning and acknowledging it in the now.

Play:

1. Be in this question, "What capacities for creating money, wealth, abundance, riches and gold do you have that you are not acknowledging that if you were to acknowledge it, would give you more money than God?"
2. Write down all your *Money Magic* stories.
3. For each *Money Magic* story say, "Wow! I created that! What would it take for me to have more of that?"

Caller: I got out a journal and started writing down every magic that I had created. It took me a little while to get it going. Yet once I started, I was amazed at what a powerful creator I am! I have created some really good stuff.

I identified 133 Money Magic Moments. I was like "Wow! And I did that!"

Another amazing story is that I wanted to do a class which cost $97. I was like, "Why does everybody else have $97? I don't even have $97." And some money just showed up in my bank account. I mean like JUST

SHOWED UP out of nowhere, like just out of thin air.

I was like "Oh wow! Wait a minute! Money, did you show up for me to get me in the class?" And it was like "Yes!" So, that's it. Money has started showing up for me already.

Nilofer: Once you start to acknowledge and to actually be present to what you are creating, you will start to see that you are creating. Every day you are creating these magical moments, every single day.

I was talking to a friend last week. She started telling me about the time that we had first met together. She said, "The first time I wanted to do a class with you, I didn't really have the money for it and I just felt I'd like to do that class." She shared a story of how money showed up for the class just because she got a client with whom she worked for the next 21 days. I was looking at her and she's telling me this happened and this happened. What she was telling me was that "I did this energetic exercise and the money showed up".

What I'd really like you to get is that it doesn't matter what you do or what you don't do, the bottom-line is that you are the one who is creating all these miracles in your life. So, when you start acknowledging what an amazing, awesome creator you are, what's going to happen is that you are going to create more and more and more of that in your life.

BARRIERS AND RECEIVING

The amount of money, riches, wealth and abundance we have depends on how much we can receive. So actually money is never a problem, it's how much we can receive. Receiving is not just about the money or material possessions. Receiving is about receiving everything, including awareness.

One of the things that stop our receiving is when we have energetic barriers and walls around us. We put up these walls to keep out bad things. However, these barriers keep out *every*thing, the bad and the good. It is only when we lower our barriers we can perceive, know, be and receive everything.

When we don't have barriers to anything, we can receive everything. When we receive everything, we have total awareness.

Every time we have a point of view or a judgment about someone or something, our energetic barriers come up. We cannot receive from behind a barrier.

Every molecule in the Universe would like to gift to us. We have all these judgments and points of view about everything; and this creates barriers.

If you hate the color red, can you receive anything from a person that wears red? Can you receive money from them? Can they become your client? No.

One of the things that I have been playing with is pushing my barriers down. It is all to do with receiving. Most of the time what happens is that as we go through life, we have our energetic barriers up. Our barriers automatically go up when we judge somebody or when we perceive someone as judging us.

What if you were consciously present and aware of when your energetic barriers are up and just noted what that is creating in your universe? When you perceive your barriers are up, push your barriers down, especially at a time in which you feel really, really, really uncomfortable. See what change that creates. Take it on as a game. What you are going to find is as your barriers remain down or as you start pushing your barriers down, you are going to be able to receive more and more and more.

Often, we think about receiving, as receiving money or receiving something physical. Yet, what if receiving was way more than that? What if receiving was all about receiving the awareness? When you are open to receiving awareness about everything with no point of view or with total allowance, I wonder what you could create in your life. Would you then be able to be aware of all those possibilities where you can create money, wealth and riches? Will you then be aware of what you need to do in order to amplify your money flows or to create wealth?

Play:

Lower all your energetic barriers. More. More. More. More. More. More. Lower any barriers you have, any walls, anywhere. Lower them. More. More. More. More. Expand to a space just outside of your body and down into Earth. Expand to a space to the size of the room you are in and down into Earth. Expand to the size of the community you are in and down into Earth. Expand to the size of the city you are in and down into Earth. Expand to the size of the country you are in and down into Earth. Expand to the size of the planet and expand beyond. Keep expanding and expanding and expanding.

Now just become aware of your feet on the floor, become aware of your bottom on the chair or wherever else your bottom is, and your hands on your thighs.

WHAT CAN I CREATE TODAY?

Now BE in this question. "What would I like to create my monetary reality as?" Just ask the question gently in your head, don't look for an answer.

Then be aware of your energetic barriers. Are they up? Or are they down? If you find your barriers going up with the words "monetary reality," what I'd like you to do is just push them down. Push your barriers down. More. More. More.

Everything the words "monetary reality" bring up for you, will you destroy and uncreate it all? Right and Wrong, Good and Bad, POD, POC, All 9, Shorts, Boys and Beyonds®

What do the words "monetary reality" mean to you? Everything that brings up will you destroy and uncreate it all? Right and Wrong, Good and Bad, POD, POC, All 9, Shorts, Boys and Beyonds®

And just push your barriers down. More. More. More. More. More.

Ask yourself, "What would I like to create my monetary reality as?"

Again, be aware of your energetic barriers. Just push your barriers down if you find them coming up.

This is exactly what happens when we hear any words to which we have judgment attached – our barriers just pop up. So all you need to do is just push your barriers down.

Ask yourself, "What would you like to create your monetary reality as?"

As you ask the question, you will perceive energy. Now get the energy of this. Just get the energy that shows up as you ask this question. Now be aware of this energy. How is this energy? Is this energy light and expansive to you? How can you perceive, know, be and receive this energy?

Get this energy in the form of a ball in front of you. Start pulling in energy from all over the universe into this ball. Keep pulling. Keep pulling. Now step up this energy. Quadruple this energy. Make it one hundred times more. Make it a godzillion times more. Receive the contribution of the universe into the energy of your monetary reality. When you start feeling light and expanded into your heart, send out trickles of energy to all those people who are looking for you from all over the universe and don't even know it. When these people find you, ask the energy to equalize so they become your repeat customers or they become people who will repeatedly contribute to your money flows.

Push down your energetic barriers even more and receive from all over the universe. Pull energy from all over the universe and send out these trickles of energy.

Now, once again, become aware of your feet on the floor, your butt sitting on the chair, and your hands on your thigh or touching your stomach and BE HERE NOW.

WHAT IS YOUR MONEY STORY?

Caller: I feel overwhelmed with a lot of demands for expenses. How does one get centered to not allow these things to overwhelm you, so that your energy does not feel like it is losing more than it is winning in order to create abundance?

Nilofer: Just lower your barriers, and lower them some more, and lower them some more. The moment you lower your barriers and you use those three points of contact – your feet on the floor, maybe your hands on your stomach, and your butt on the chair or your back against the chair, or anything like that; you will be totally present, totally here in this moment. The moment that happens, all this energy of overwhelm or anything else that is going on in your universe, you will find that you are here now. You are totally present with whatever is going on in your life. You are also in the space of no judgment or total allowance.

JOY AND MONEY

Caller: When I was younger, like in my twenties, I would select or do things from the energy of excitement or something. I would just come up with ways to make it happen. However, now, at this point of my life, I have made so many mistakes around money and suffered the consequences that I now don't really trust myself. Now all my decisions are made from the standpoint of "Do I have the money now?" Right now, I don't have the money. I feel stuck and frustrated, because I can't do what I want to do. As a result, I am constantly struggling with a lack of money. My whole life has become "How can I generate and actualize more money, so that I can meet my living expenses each month?" There is no fun or joy in this way of living. So, the question is, "how can I trust myself and how can I generate an abundance of money each month?"

Nilofer: Everything that is, will you destroy and uncreate it all? Right and Wrong, Good and Bad, POD, POC, All 9, Shorts, Boys and Beyonds®

Everything that your money story is, will you destroy and uncreate it all? Right and Wrong, Good and Bad, POD, POC, All 9, Shorts, Boys and Beyonds®

How many points of view and judgments are you using to keep your money story in place? Everything that doesn't allow you to perceive, know, be and receive that, will you destroy and uncreate it all? Right and Wrong, Good and Bad, POD, POC, All 9, Shorts, Boys and Beyonds®

How many points of view and judgments do you have that are restricting your money flows? Everything that is, times godzillion, will you destroy and uncreate it all? Right and Wrong, Good and Bad, POD, POC, All 9, Shorts, Boys and Beyonds®

Basically, what I would do is keep destroying and un-creating all your points of view about your money stories. Every time you feel this constriction about your money, your finances and your monetary reality, just POD and POC. I can perceive the energy which is in this question, which is like "Wow! It is so loaded!" If you could just write out your money story, keep looking at it, and just keep POCing and PODing everything that shows up as you are reading your money story, you will clear a lot of your points of view.

One of the things which I always like to tell people is that you have the tools. Use them. I have seen that money is one of the easiest things to change with Access. When I started my Access journey, I said "the best way in which I see these tools work is my money situation." I started using all the tools of Access to change my whole money situation. In three months, I could literally see that I had started from zero and was way up.

TOOLS TO CREATE MONEY AND GET OUT OF DEBT

Caller: I have created my finances to perpetuate struggle. I have been months behind on my household bills for the past year. I also have 40k in debt I haven't paid on since 2008. I do not spend money on my body, make-up, clothes, shoes, gifts for occasions, furniture, autos or fun. I do not choose to spend money on things that would be fun for me as I'm so far behind on my bills and debts. I'm scraping by. What would it take for me to move forward with ease of money, be ahead on all my bills and pay all my debts?

Nilofer: This is a great question and I can go in ten different ways with it. Everything that brings up will you destroy and uncreate it all? Right and Wrong, Good and Bad, POD, POC, All 9, Shorts, Boys and Beyonds®

The first thing I would do is ask "**What's right about all this I'm not getting?**" Get out of the wrongness of whatever is going on in your monetary reality. Every time you become aware of going into constriction with your monetary reality, ask "What's right about this I'm not getting?"

I will share with you a few tools. Look at each tool and use it. Use these tools in your life. There are times when I will hear Gary Douglas, the founder of Access Consciousness®, say something. And I'll think "Wow! That sounds great, but oh my God, I can't use that in my life". The moment I go to that place, I go to POC and POD. And I will say "What will it take for me to use that tool in my life?" It's as simple as asking a question. If you play with all the tools that I'm going to share with you, it will start to create more in your life.

The first tool is the "**10 percent account**". Start to set aside 10 percent of every penny that comes into your bank account or everything that you earn into your "**I have money**" account. Basically what happens is that we get money and then that money goes away. So, you have the money coming in and you have the money going out. It's almost like you keep seeing the money coming in and going out. Every time you see money in your bank account or in your wallet, the thoughts that are going through your mind are, "but I have to use this money to pay this, this, this, this, this and this."

If you have a huge debt (we refer to debts as past expenditures in Access Consciousness®), it's almost like this past expenditure is sitting there like this huge boulder on your head.

To create your "I have money" account, it can be a bank account you create, it can be an envelope in which you are putting in money and put it under your mattress, or you can just carry this in a compartment in your wallet. What you do is you start putting 10 percent of every dollar or any money you receive into this "I have money" account. You are never ever going to spend this money.

You don't spend this money at all. Basically what starts to happen is that slowly this account is going to start growing. I started my account when I was not earning anything. Nothing was coming in. My husband would give me an amount of money for household expenses. I started taking out 10 percent of that money and putting it away in my "I have money" account. In one and a half years, it has grown a hundred fold. When you start putting away money into your "I have money" account for a period of a few months; you will realize "Oh, I have money. I have money. I have money." That starts to create a totally different energy in your universe. That energy will start to contribute to your money flows. Don't ever take money out of your "I have money" account. If you have to take out money from this account, look at it like a loan that you are giving yourself. Take it out. Then first thing you do is put it back again.

The other thing you have to do is not pay your bills first. Put money in your "I have money" account first. Look at it as "No, I'm not touching this and the remaining money is what I have to pay with." Think of it in this way, "Are you honoring you? Or are you honoring your bills?" Now this itself will create a huge shift in your universe.

The second thing that you do is to **carry a big sum of money in your purse** (or wallet or billfold), which makes you feel like a wealthy person. If you are just starting out, begin by carrying your "I have money" account in your purse until it becomes so huge that you have to literally transfer it somewhere. It could be a $100 bill or it could be any amount of money that makes you feel like a rich person. **But, don't spend that money.** Just carry that money with you all the time. This also has an amazing expansive energy to it.

A few months ago, my "I have money" account grew so big that I could literally not carry that amount of cash in my purse. So I removed it and put it away somewhere else. It just slipped my mind about carrying this big sum of money in my purse. Then I started noticing that I had this deficit going on with money until one day I realized "Oh, so that's what changed in my purse." Again, I've started carrying this huge amount of money in my purse. Carry whatever is a huge amount of money for you. You will start to notice things shift for you.

The third thing that you could start doing is **setting aside a small sum of money which is going as payment towards your past expenditure(s)**. It could be as small as $5 or $10. Every time you make the payment towards your past expenditure, say "Thank you Universe" and "What would it take for me to make this payment with total ease, joy and glory?" "What would it take for me to pay a hundred times this?" Just question. Even if it is a small payment of $5 or $10, it gets you started with that energy. Then start asking the universe to contribute to it.

The other one that you could also use is "What energy, space and consciousness can my body and I be to pay off our past expenditures with total ease, joy and glory? Everything that doesn't allow me to perceive, know, be and receive that, will I destroy and uncreate it all? Right and Wrong, Good and Bad, POD, POC, All 9, Shorts, Boys and Beyonds®'"

The fourth thing is to **set aside a small sum of money for you to have fun with**. It could be whatever amount you can take out. It could be $10, $20, or $50. Set aside this amount for you every month. This is your fun money. Go out and have fun with this money. Use this money to nurture your body. That's how you bring in the energy of fun with your money.

Just play with these tools. You have to remember that there is no fixed fix to anything, but if you start using the tools and consistently start using them in your life over and over and over again, things will start to shift and change for you.

Use the clearings and start taking physical action on these things. Once again, look at the tools that you want to play with and start asking the question "What would it take for me to use these tools?" That question has magic to it and it just starts to create some amazing stuff.

ENERGY OF CREATION OF MONEY

Caller: We have used a lot of different tools over the years and had a period of time where we actually created a lot of money and put some of it aside. You know, maybe 10 percent, then a little bit more in the special account, but we are just in this space right now where we are just not creating any money. And so we have the money that we created and that's put aside. And then we have our bank account, which just seems to be going down and down and down. I know that there's a way to create more money and I'm just wondering at what point -- I mean, do you NEVER tap into the money that you put aside in your 10 percent account? Because I guess some of the things that are running through my mind are like "Whoa! The bank account is going down. Am I going to have to tap into my 10 percent account?" I just wanted some thoughts around that or some tools.

Nilofer: That's such a great question. You've created a lot of money and then you've also created this phase where you had no money after that showing up. Do not touch your "I have money" account. What I would ask you is "Are you creating money? Are you creating money right now?" We create a lot of money. Then we go to this place of like "Wow! That's the best!!!" Can you then out-create that? You cannot then, because you have judged this to be the best 'X-Y-Z' in your life.

So everything that brings up, will you destroy and uncreate it all? Right and Wrong, Good and Bad, POD, POC, All 9, Shorts, Boys and Beyonds®

What I'd like you to do is get the energy when you were creating that money. Perceive that energy. Who created that money? You did. So apparently you have capacity for creating money. That energy you just perceived, allow that energy to contribute to your money flows. Just push down your energetic barriers. Push them down and just allow that energy to contribute to your life, your living, your body, your money flows and your future.

You have to be in this energy of creation of money. For a lot of people, there's a laid back energy as if you are doing something really heavy. But what if you were to just play with that energy? What if you were to go "Oh, I wonder how I could create money today?" or "What is the space for me to create money today?" Start playing with that energy. Whatever you have created in your life, just tap into that energy and allow it to contribute to your money flows, contribute to your body, and contribute to any part of your life. When you start doing that, it's like that energy is available to us. You could use it and play with it.

Then use that tool "be in the question". You could ask "I wonder what it would take to make XYZ money show up?" "What can I add to my life today to have XYZ amount of money to show up right away?" Being in those questions and being in that playful energy will start to create more in your life. If you go into deficit, just POD and POC it.

FEAR AND WORRY ABOUT MONEY

Caller: How can I get over this worry that comes up when I don't have immediate money coming in? I would prefer to not get a 9 to 5 job, but I also don't know where the money will come from if I don't.

Nilofer: Fear and worry are Distractor Implants. Distractor Implants are a lie. They put your attention on something you cannot handle. Every time you have the worry come up, remember it's just a distractor implant. Say "All the distractor implants of anxiety and worries, destroy and uncreate it all. Everything underneath it, keeping it in place destroy and uncreate it all. Right and Wrong, Good and Bad, POD, POC, All 9, Shorts, Boys and Beyonds® Catch yourself in that moment and just POD and POC the distractor implant of worry and everything underneath that distractor implant keeping it in place.

The other thing you do, the action item that you do is ask "What can I add to my life today to have money coming in right away?"

Be in this question. How many judgments do you have about not taking a 9 to 5 job? Everything that is, will you destroy and uncreate it all? Right and Wrong, Good and Bad, POD, POC, All 9, Shorts, Boys and Beyonds® Because it's almost like you are saying "I will have money coming in this way, but I will not have money coming in via a 9 to 5 job because the 9 to 5 job is boring."

Why do you want to cut off your receiving in that way? What if you could be open to all the possibilities that are available to you? What if you could get an amazing job doing something that you love to do and it may be 9 to 5, it may not be 9 to 5, whatever is possible?

All the points of view that you have that are restricting your money flows, will you destroy and uncreate it all? Right and Wrong, Good and Bad, POD, POC, All 9, Shorts, Boys and Beyonds®

When you start being the question "What can I add to my life today to have money coming in right away?" it's almost like you will start to see these possibilities pop up in your universe. When these possibilities pop up you go and take action.

What happened for me, I was looking at creating my classes and I had not been getting a lot of numbers coming in to my Access classes. So I started being in this question – "What can I add to my life today to have more people coming in to my classes right away?" I have been in this question. I just had these awarenesses of "I have to create these beautiful brochures." So I created these beautiful brochures which look very amazing. And they just pull people. I laid out those brochures where I taught my Access classes. That brochure was lying on the reception. This woman comes in, she's talking about something else, and then her eyes go to the brochure. She picked up the brochure, started reading it. All this got created because I was in that question "So what can I add to my life today to have more people coming in to my classes right away?" And the thing is, when you be in the question, you will have the awarenesses. Then just follow the energies. Take action.

CREATING AND EXPANDING

Caller: How do you keep creating and expanding with ease after you have received the money you've asked for? I find that I receive, then stop and then get in the same situation again.

Nilofer: You have to keep asking for more, keep expanding your asking. Say you've asked for XYZ, even as you will start to see that the XYZ is actualizing in your universe, start asking for something more. Ask for two things more to show up when you can see one is in the process of being actualized. We all get into this space, but keep asking for more and more and more. So as one thing starts getting actualized, ask for two to show up. If you keep following that, you will never get into that situation again.

Caller: I tend to create lots of money but then over time I spend it, even my "I have money" account. What will it take to actually have money and not just spend it?

Nilofer: Create money. Keep asking for more to show up. You will remain in that energy of creating more and more and more money. And please whatever you do, don't touch your "I have money" account.

CREATING YOUR MONETARY REALITY

Caller: When you ask the question, I feel anxiety. Do I push that down? The question that gave me anxiety was "What would I like to create my monetary reality as?"

Nilofer: When you ask that question and have anxiety show up, you have to be in this question "What does my monetary reality mean to me?" Everything that is times godzillion destroy and uncreate it all. Right and Wrong, Good and Bad, POD, POC, All 9, Shorts, Boys and Beyonds®

You have some points of view that you are attaching to the words "monetary reality." You have some judgment or maybe you have some judgments about creating your monetary reality when you are wondering "Oh my God, how do I create my monetary reality?"

Use this clearing over and over again: What does creating my monetary reality mean to me? Everything that is times godzillion destroy and uncreate it all. Right and Wrong, Good and Bad, POD, POC, All 9, Shorts, Boys and Beyonds®

Keep asking this question over and over and over again until you have no charge. Then you ask "What would I like to create my monetary reality as?"

One of the things that I noticed for myself is that I found myself comparing myself to other people who are doing what I do. I started looking at

"Oh my God, they have these many people showing up in their classes, which means they must be making this amount of money. I just have these many people and I'm not making that money."

There is that little thing called judgment, which I'm sure none of you do. I started doing that and I realized then what my monetary reality was. That means what is real to me about the monetary reality in my universe. For example, maybe there is somebody who has been in business for many, many years and they have a totally different reality for them. One hundred thousand dollars is like small change for them, and they would like to create maybe $1 million or maybe $50 million or whatever. Maybe there is another person whose monetary reality is a yearly income of $10,000 and they would like to expand their monetary reality. If they were to judge themselves or compare themselves to this one hundred thousand dollar person, all that they are going to do is to create a deficit in their universe.

Look at where you are at right now with your money situation. Ask for two, three or four times that to show up. Ask for what is ease, joy and glory for you, and is not going to feel heavy for you. Start asking for more money to show up. For example, I'm looking at creating classes. At one point I was being in this question of "What can I add to my life to have 10 people showing up in my classes right away?" Then after I was in that question for 2 or 3 days, it just expanded. Ten people felt too constricted for me. So I started asking for 20 people to show up. And after doing that for a few days, I asked "What can I add to my life to have hundreds of people showing up in my classes right away?" That does not mean that I have hundreds in my classes right now. What you have to remember is that we are creating for a future. We are creating now for a future. Hundreds of people energy is a really light and expansive energy for me to play with. "What can I add in my life today to create hundreds of people showing up for my classes right away that's fun for me."

All the points of view we have about creating a monetary reality, just start

POCing and PODing that. Then be in the question "What would I like to create my monetary reality as?"

When you are in that question and when you have that expansive energy show up, (oftentimes, I won't even know what that expansive energy is) things will start to shift and change in my universe. Things will start to show up which are totally magical, which I could never ever have dreamed possible for me.

"The future that could exist is far greater than the future you can imagine."- Gary Douglas.

Caller: We have to be able to receive from anywhere too. What questions would you ask to get that in place?

Nilofer: I have been sharing this question and the biggest thing I would say is, push down your energetic barriers. When you have your barriers down, you are able to actually receive from everything. Right now, as you are going throughout the day, just be aware of your barriers. Maybe you could put a "Barriers?" reminder in your phone that pops up every hour. Then you ask "Do I have my barriers up? Do I have my barriers down? What is that creating in my life? And if my barriers are up, I wonder what will happen if I push them down?" Just push your barriers down. So, every hour if you have a reminder showing up on your phone and if you were to push your barriers down, I wonder how much receiving that would create in your universe!

HOW TO BECOME MONEY WORKBOOK 100X

Do 100X to Get 100 Million ~ Gary Douglas
This is what Gary wrote for me when he autographed my
Money workbook.
I am on a mission to do the Money Workbook 100X. Join me
http://www.moneycirclebook.com

CHAPTER TWO

RECEIVING

"Magic Is About Receiving" Gary Douglas

In his book, *Money Isn't the Problem, You Are*, written by Gary Douglas, the founder of Access Consciousness®, he writes it's rarely a money problem. It is a problem with receiving.

One of the things we don't do very well in this reality is to receive. When we look at the word receiving, what we are likely thinking about is receiving material, physical, concrete things like receiving money. But if you actually expand this whole concept of receiving, ultimate receiving is actually receiving awareness. So if you are receiving awareness, if you have total awareness, would you then have awareness about all the possibilities where you can create or generate money? Of course, yes! For example, you are going through your day and you walk into a place, you could receive awareness about all the money and all the possibilities of money that exist in that place with ultimate receiving.

One way in which we actually turn off our receiving is to put up all these energetic barriers around us. And the funny part is that most of the time, we are not even aware that we are putting up barriers around us.

What are energetic barriers? Energetic barriers are like these walls that we place around ourselves. We place these barriers around ourselves when we want to protect ourselves, like when we have been hurt. The problem with barriers is that not only do they keep out all the bad things; they may also keep out all the things that we desire. So what I'd like to do right now is to take you through a little exercise so that you can get an awareness of all the barriers you have around you.

You can close your eyes during this exercise or you can keep your eyes open. Think about and be present to your energetic barriers, to all the walls that you have around yourself. Be present to how you perceive your energetic barriers. Just perceive and know what these barriers feel like to you. Perceive what kind of sensations they are creating in your body. Now what I'd like you to do is just push down these barriers. How do you push down these barriers? Just by asking. It's as simple as that.

Ask and you shall receive.

Push down your barriers. And push down your barriers even more. Push them down even more. More. More. More. Push your barriers down even more. More. More. More. Push them down more in any universes, anywhere and everywhere you have your energetic barriers up. Just push them down. More. More. More. More. More. More. More. More. And now how does that feel to you?

Now I'd like you to be aware of a place in nature. Maybe it is a beautiful forest or maybe you are just walking on the grass with beautiful trees, flowers and plants around you. Now perceive your energetic barriers. Do you have them up? Or do you have them down? Now, just for a minute, push your barriers up. What does that feels like? Now push your barriers down. What does that feel like?

Now be aware of a city where you have all these tall buildings surrounding you. Do you have your barriers up or do you have your barriers down? Push your barriers up here to perceive what that feels like for you. Push your barriers down and perceive what that feels like for you. Are you receiving more when you have your barriers up or when you have your barriers down? What are you receiving? Are you receiving the energy? Are you receiving awareness? How does it feel when you have your barriers down?

Now be aware of this beautiful pool of water. Dip your toes in the water, and then go for a swim in the water. Perceive your energetic barriers. Do you have your barriers up? Or do have your barriers down? And when you have your barriers down, what does that feel like? If you have your barriers up, just push them down.

Now be aware of this beautiful shop which is filled with gold, jewels, antiques and all kinds of beautiful things. Push your barriers up in this shop and perceive what that feels like. Now push your barriers down. Perceive what that feels like to be surrounded by all this gold, diamonds and beautiful jewelry. Just keep pushing your barriers down.

Now think about the most expensive, opulent and luxurious shop that you know of. Do you have your barriers up? Or do have your barriers down? And if you have your barriers up, just push them down. Perceive what it feels like to be in this beautiful, opulent, luxurious shop with your barriers down. I wonder what you can receive from this place when you have your barriers down. Can you allow the energy of gold, diamonds and all this beautiful jewelry to contribute to your life, your living, your money flows and your bank account?

Now think about a place where you feel really uncomfortable. Do you have your barriers up or your barriers down? If you have your barriers up, just push your barriers down. Now perceive what it feels like to have your barriers down in this place, which you never liked before.

Now perceive a garbage dump or a toxic waste site. Do you have your barriers up or your barriers down? Push your barriers down. Perceive what it feels like to have your barriers down in this place. What if you were not to label it as a toxic waste or garbage dump? Would you perceive it as free-flowing energy? What if it was just free-flowing energy? Could you use this energy? Could this energy be a contribution to your life, your living, your reality, your money flows and your bank accounts?

Are you receiving more when you have your energetic barriers up or when you have your barriers down? How many points of view do you have about where and when you are going to receive?

Now think about being in your favorite restaurant where you are enjoying the most delicious, nurturing food for your body. Do you have your barriers up or your barriers down? And if you have your barriers up, just push them down. How does that feel to you?

Now think about the time when you ate in a restaurant and your body didn't enjoy it so much. Did you have your barriers up at that point of time? Or did you have your barriers down? Just push down your barriers. When you have your barriers down, did it change the energy you were experiencing at that point of time?

Now I'd like you to think about being in a crowded marketplace. Do you have your energetic barriers up? Or do you have your barriers down? If you have your barriers up, push them down. Does anything change for you being in that marketplace when you have your barriers down?

Now think about being in your own home. Do you have your barriers up? Or do you have your barriers down? If you have your barriers up, just push them down. What information can you receive? What energy and what contribution can you receive from your own home? How would being in your home change when you have your energetic barriers down when you are at home?

Now think about going grocery shopping to your favorite grocery store. Do you have your barriers up or your barriers down? Push your barriers down. What information can you receive from everything around you? I wonder how your shopping would change if you were to be there with your barriers down. Would you get information about things that are nurturing to your body? Would you get information about special deals and prices? And what else would be possible here?

Now think about flying first class or business class in a plane. Do you have your barriers up to that? If you do, lower your barriers. What contribution could that be to your body?

Now think about being in this luxurious hotel where you are surrounded by all these beautiful things. Do you let your barriers go up here or do they go down? Just be aware. And if you have your barriers up, just push your barriers down. What would it be like to live in this beautiful place for a month?

Now I'd like you to be in this question: "What would I like to create my monetary reality as?" Get the energy of it. What amount of money would be fun for you to have in your life? Whatever money you would like to create, keep that figure in your awareness. Do you have your barriers up or your barriers down to that? If you have your barriers up, push them down. What would it be like to have $1 million? What would it take for you to have $1 million? Does this question put up your barriers? If your barriers are up, push them down.

What if creating anything is "ask and you shall receive" and the only thing stopping you from receiving is the barriers you have in place? Every time you ask for something, be aware of your barriers. Do you have your barriers up or your barriers down? If you have your energetic barriers up, just push them down. Then be aware of what that creates in your universe.

Play around with this tool. I'd like you to just be aware of your energetic barriers all day long. What happens when you have your barriers up?

What happens when you have your barriers down? There's no right or wrong, good or bad with this. It's simply for you to be aware of what it creates in your universe when you have your barriers up and when you have your barriers down.

How much fun can we have today? How much money can we create, generate and actualize today? Everything that doesn't allow that will you destroy and uncreate it all? Right and Wrong, Good and Bad, POD, POC, All 9, Shorts, Boys and Beyonds®

SPACE

Caller: What came up for me were questions about allowing as well as receiving. It seems like there is a lot of information coming in from different places. So, I'm not quite sure what questions to ask. When I lower all my barriers, it's like not an overflow of information. Yet sometimes it's coming from different places, and I'm not sure what to do next.

Nilofer: When you have the kind of feeling of not expansion and if you are aware of something, you could go to the questions, "What is this? What can I do with it? Can I change this? How can I change this?"

I live in this community in the middle of the desert. I go for a walk everyday along these beautiful trails that are there. The other day, there were a couple of men who were hanging out there. As I was walking, I just perceived this really weird energy. I lowered my barriers and realized I was judging me for not being able to lower my barriers. When I experienced that, I went to question and asked, "What is this? What can I do with it? Can I change it? And, how can I change it?" The moment I went to those questions, I became aware that those men had so much judgment in their universe. The moment I had that awareness, I asked, "Is this relevant to me?" It wasn't. Then this energy just kind of lightened up for me.

The other thing you can do is expand out. How far do you need to expand out to be at ease with this?

ENERGY PULLS

Caller: The only other thing that comes up is about money and receiving money from other areas. I always wondered whether the time was right and what I needed to ask or say to this person to receive more money in business. Not as payment for my services, but to have them pay more.

Nilofer: There's this exercise which is called the "Energy Pull" that's really easy. When you are with people who are your customers or even on an everyday basis, push down your energetic barriers. Then push them down even more. Then expand to the size of the room you are in and down into Earth. Expand to the size of the building you are in and down into Earth. Expand to the size of the community you live in and down into Earth. Expand to the size of the city you are in and down into Earth. Expand to the size of the country you are in and down into Earth. Expand to the size of Earth, and keep expanding and expanding.

Then place the energy of your business in front of you. "What would you like to create your business as? What is the minimum income you would like to have? How many clients you would like to see in a week or in a month?" Just get that energy in front of you and start pulling in energies from all over the universe into that energy. Keep pulling more and more of that energy, and send out trickles of energy to all those people who are looking for you and don't even know it.

Allow those trickles of energy to equalize when those people find you. Make asking "How can I get more money from the usual customers I have?" one of the questions that you can be in. From what you said caller, it's almost like you are constricting your universe with your customers. If you start asking for more and more people to show up, and start playing with this energy exercise every day in the morning; you will notice that you will be adding more and more to your business. One of the questions I love and I've been playing around with is "What can I add to my business today to have more customers or new clients show up right away?" or "What can I add to my business today to have more clients show up right away?" Just play with that.

BODY AND RECEIVING

Caller: I have things in my home, antiques and such, that for years I have wanted to sell. I now realize that for my health and well-being, I must leave my home shortly and start some place that does not have the smart-meters on the property. I'm having mine replaced soon and have ordered an analog meter to replace the smart one. However, the town where I live is a home community. My neighbors all have them, and I can't make them replace theirs. There are over 274, all very close together to each other. So the energy is more condensed. And I apparently am sensitive to them and having side-effects, because they collect together and the energy is not visible.

Nilofer: If you have something that is affecting your body, then the best thing to do is to ask "Body, how can we have more ease with this?" and "Body, where would you like to live and what would it take for us to create that?" The thing with money and abundance is a lot of it is related, because the things we buy with money are for our body. We could ask for contribution from our body to that. "Body, what contribution can you be for us to have greater ease with all this?"

I love to receive The Bars® and bodywork. (Access Body Classes invite you to the greatness of receiving the energies you have available through and with your body. Whether taking a 3-Day Body Class or just one class focusing on a single Body Process, your body will be sure to thank you.) I had a really interesting point of view that I live out of the city and so don't have anyone with whom I can swap sessions. Until one fine day I asked, "Body, what would it take for us to receive more and more of The

Bars® and bodyworks?" Since then I've connected with a bunch of people. Now I swap The Bars® and bodywork three or four times a week, which is amazing to my body! Whatever you need for your body, ask for your body's contribution to that.

You could also run a clearing for this. "What energy, space and consciousness can my body and I be to be at greater ease with all of this for all eternity? Everything that doesn't allow it, destroy and uncreate it all. Right and Wrong, Good and Bad, POD, POC, All 9, Shorts, Boys and Beyonds®"

When you think "I really need to sell all these things that I have to lighten my life and have less stuff," how many points of view and judgments do you have with that? Have you already judged that you have too many things in your home and you need to lighten it? Everything that is, will you destroy and uncreate it all? Right and Wrong, Good and Bad, POD, POC, All 9, Shorts, Boys and Beyonds®

What if you could look at everything in your home, which you "think" is clutter, and ask it, "Are you a contribution in my life?" If the energy is expansive, then ask another question, "Would you like to still own me?" Because we think we own our possessions, yet the opposite is true. Actually, the possessions own us. So ask it "Would you like to own me?" If you get a "no" on it, then you ask "Who else would you like to own? Can you please find that person?"

Every molecule in the universe would like to contribute to us. We can ask everything to contribute to us. You can ask for a contribution from everything that is in your life. And you can ask for their contribution in whatever way you would like it. Just ask. One more thing, remember to lower your barriers. Expand out. Become aware of your home and everything in your home. If you find your energetic barriers coming up, just push them down some more. Then ask for everything that is in your space to contribute to your life, your living, your reality, your money flows, your body and your future. Perceive the energy of the contribution. When you have your barriers down, you will actually start to receive information from everything in your home including those things which no longer wish to own you. So just ask them to find a new owner. It's as simple as that.

Caller: I need help fast. The powers that be at work are putting more pressure to produce more work. This work is no longer in alignment with me, so I started my own business. There's movement, but no money coming in. I would like to receive money, so that I can quit. Help!

Nilofer: If you have a timeline at which you are operating, that doesn't really work. What you have to do is find out how much ease can you be in your workplace.

You could use this clearing. "What energy, space and consciousness can my body and I be to create greater ease in my workplace? Everything that doesn't allow that, will I destroy and uncreate it all? Right and Wrong, Good and Bad, POD, POC, All 9, Shorts, Boys and Beyonds®"

When you have this thing of "I would like to receive the money", it's almost like a projection, an expectation that "I've created this business. And so I will have the new money coming in and then I can quit my job." When you have all those points of view around it, how much are you actually going to create?

Here's another good clearing. All the projections, expectations, separations, rejections and judgement that you have around your business, now and in the future, will you destroy and uncreate it all? Right and Wrong, Good and Bad, POD, POC, All 9, Shorts, Boys and Beyonds®

Destroy and uncreate your job and your business every single day so you don't carry over from the next day whatever was going on. Ask for contribution from your business. "Business, what can you contribute to me today and what can I contribute to you today?" Ask "Job, what can you contribute to me today and what can I contribute to you today?"

CONTRIBUTION

Contribution is always the simultaneity of gifting and receiving.

The other thing is how many barriers do you have up to your job that you have this constriction going on in your universe? Just become aware of your job and push down your barriers. Then push your energetic barriers down even more. Become aware of the energy of pressure. Is it still the same? Is it still the same or has it changed just by pushing your barriers down? If you can just be aware of that energy, that is free energy. It's like we judge energy. We say, "Oh my God, this is pressure. This is anxiety." It is like we feel sick, so we put all these labels to energy. What if you were to let go of all the labels? Let go of all the labels and you will perceive the energy as being different. That energy is free energy, and it is available for you to use.

You can look at different areas of your life and say, "I'd like to contribute that energy to my business, or I'd like to contribute that energy to my relationship." It's almost like that energy is infinite. As you are contributing that energy to your business, perceive how your business is contributing back to you. Is that energy expanding even more? Now take that energy and contribute it to your body. Then perceive the contribution from your body, adding on to that energy. Now take that energy and contribute it to your relationship. Allow your relationship to contribute to you. And that energy is expanding and expanding and expanding. You'll realize how much free energy you have. Look at the different projects that you have and start contributing energy to all the projects that you have. Then perceive the energy of receiving from all those projects. Contribute the energy to your money flows. Perceive the simultaneity of receiving from all your money flows.

JOY AND HAPPINESS

Caller: This may sound stupid. I'm scared about having fun. So guess what? I create no fun in my life. I do my best to not isolate and hide. I seem to have lost the capacity to truly laugh and enjoy life. My body has been crying so much. I totally cannot face being with others, and being called a "wimp" shuts me down so much. I'm doing my best that I seem to be able to be.

Nilofer: What does being a wimp mean to you? Everything that it is will you destroy and uncreate it all? Right and Wrong, Good and Bad, POD, POC, All 9, Shorts, Boys and Beyonds®

Now push down your barriers to yourself and expand out. Think about being just with one person. If you feel your barriers coming up, just push them down. Now think about being with five people. Once again, if you feel your barriers coming up, push them down. Now think about being with ten people and push down any of your barriers which have come up. Now think about being with fifty people and push down all the barriers which have come up. Think about being with one hundred people and push down the barriers that spring up. Now be with five hundred people and push down your barriers even more. Now, be with five thousand people and push down your barriers even more. Now, be with a hundred thousand people and push down your barriers. Now, what I'd like you to do is to tap into the energy of Earth. Then pull up the energy of Earth through your feet, through your body, filling your whole body and expanding out into the universe and beyond.

Tap into the energy of joy, happiness, fun and laughter. Start pulling in energy from all over the universe, and from Earth into your body. Then allow it to flow out of your body and expand out into the universe.

You could ask "How much fun could I have today?" Ask your body to contribute to the fun. "Body, what can we do today that will create a lot of fun for us today?" "How much fun, laughter, joy and happiness can we have today?"

ARE YOU AN EFFECT OF OTHER PEOPLE?

Caller: How do I not allow my significant other's emotional response to not stop me when I desire something that costs more than what he's thinking it ought to cost, like a workshop, which is not something he does. He eventually gets okay with it. It just takes a lot of energy on my part to get through. Inside I often feel sick. My solar plexus gets hurt. I get a burning sensation, and I'm not even being able to eat. I've been told that it's so, so selfish. So I accommodated. Even as a child, I didn't need anything. I went without food sometimes."

Nilofer: Everything that brings up, will you destroy and uncreate it all? Right and Wrong, Good and Bad, POD, POC, All 9, Shorts, Boys and Beyonds®

All the points of view keeping all of that in place and all the decisions, judgements, conclusions, computations, keeping all of that in place, will you destroy and uncreate it all? Right and Wrong, Good and Bad, POD, POC, All 9, Shorts, Boys and Beyonds®

One of the things I have noticed is that by lowering my barriers all the time, especially when I am with people, I find that it creates so much ease in my universe by just being with people and just being in that space of total allowance. Another thing is to also have allowance for your significant other's point of view or everybody else's point of view about money. What you've got to get is that they are functioning from a limited point of view with money. They are functioning from a finite point of view with money, a constriction with money. Do you function from that constriction with money too?

You don't. You actually function with such an infinite perspective with money. Then you have all these people around you who have such a finite and constricted perspective of money. Then you go "They are all functioning from that place and then I don't understand why they are like that." So you start biomimetically mimicking them. (The main element of understanding is referred to as Biomimetic Mimicry. Biomimetic Mimicry is what you lock into the body trying to duplicate or understand others. It is the natural ability of the body to be able to fit in the rest of the world.) You buy into their reality with money and lock it in place in your body.

What creation are you using to invoke and perpetrate the biomimetic and biomimetric mimicry of other people's pain, pathways and realities with money are you choosing? Everything that is times godzillion will you destroy and uncreate it all? Right and Wrong, Good and Bad, POD, POC, All 9, Shorts, Boys and Beyonds®

Keep running this process on yourself more and more. You will start to notice that you begin to unlock all that from your universe, which will allow you more ease being present with what your reality with money actually is.

There's something more here. What also happens is that if it's coming from when you were a child, then you are also mimicking your mother and your father.

What creation are you using to invoke and perpetrate the biomimetic and biomimetric mimicry of your mother's pain, pathways and reality with money are you choosing? Everything that is times godzillion will you destroy and uncreate it all? Right and Wrong, Good and Bad, POD, POC, All 9, Shorts, Boys and Beyonds®

What creation are you using to invoke and perpetrate the biomimetic and biomimetric mimicry of your father's pain, pathways and reality with money are you choosing? Everything that is times godzillion will you destroy and uncreate it all? Right and Wrong, Good and Bad, POD, POC, All 9, Shorts, Boys and Beyonds®

Lower your barriers. Now be with your significant other. If your barriers come up, just lower your barriers. Now think about asking them for money. If your barriers come up, just push them down. It's as easy as that. The more you practice pushing your barriers down, you'll notice that everything becomes a lot more easy in the universe.

IF MONEY WERE NOT THE ISSUE WHAT WOULD YOU CHOOSE?

Caller: Hi. I have been aware lately that I have been in the waiting room of my life. I am so willing to stop waiting, and truly create a life of fun, joy and ease. It seems not possible when there are money issues. I fear how money is not the issue. So how does one clear this? I've always put self on hold. Something talks me out of purchasing even clothes to wear that are required. I will wear something till it falls apart or shabby.

Nilofer: Every time you go to purchase something and you have this energy comes up for you, just ask "If money were not the issue, what would I choose? Everything that brings up, will you destroy and uncreate it all? Right and Wrong, Good and Bad, POD, POC, All 9, Shorts, Boys and Beyonds®" And push your barriers down to receiving everything.

When you start asking this question, you will actually start making choices not based on money.

The thing that we are afraid of is that if we do not choose based on money, then we will end up spending a lot of money. What you've got to get is that you are an infinite being. See yourself as an infinite being who has total awareness of your future. You are only going to make choices which are going to expand your future, if you start functioning from an infinite being. Often when I be in that question "If money were not the issue, what would I choose?", when I have to make that choice, even though in the short-term it feels like it's going to pinch me to buy that thing, and I ask the question; I get an awareness of what I'd like to choose. I get an awareness of the energy that it's going to create. It usually turns out that it will not be the most expensive choice. Yet I will get so much information about what that choice is going to create, it will expand my universe.

STOP AND START

Caller: I'm aware that every month I make enough money to pay bills and rent, and even at the end of the month I'm rushing to get the money together to pay the rent. And I do get it. I'm tired of being in the dark end every month. I do some clearings on this, but it seems I get comfortable. Does this mean that I stop creating or I'm not willing to receive more, even though I sense I'm very good to attract money in my life?

Nilofer: What creation are you using to invoke and perpetrate the start and end of every month you are choosing? Everything that is times godzillion will you destroy and uncreate it all? Right and Wrong, Good and Bad, POD, POC, All 9, Shorts, Boys and Beyonds®

What have you made so vital about possessing, that you would create the start and end every month in order to have it? Everything that is times godzillion will you destroy and uncreate it all? Right and Wrong, Good and Bad, POD, POC, All 9, Shorts, Boys and Beyonds®

And then you can be in the question, "What can I add to my life today to have more money right away?" and "What can I be or do different today to have more money right away?"

Money is a creation. How much are you contributing to your money flows every single day? How much are you creating your money flows every single day? Being in the question and following the energy when it shows up will start to create more and more money in your life.

One of my personal things that I do is when I start a project and midway, I'll start three more projects. It's almost like I'm creating all the time. When you are creating all the time, you will always have that flow of energy, the gifting and receiving of energy and money.

Earlier I would be doing just one thing and went about finding more and more clients. Now I do it different. I have multiple streams of income. So if one stream is not working that well, I will have some different stream flowing in at all points of time. I don't go into that place of being constricted by my money flows.

Here's another clearing you can use: What can I be or do different today to create multiple streams of income in my life and my business right away? Everything that doesn't allow that will you destroy and uncreate it all? Right and Wrong, Good and Bad, POD, POC, All 9, Shorts, Boys and Beyonds®

ATTENDING CLASSES

Caller: Is there a clearing, specifically, if I would like to attend a class in Florida? In this ten seconds it would require flight, hotels, food, clothing—summer clothing—and class expenses.

Nilofer: First go and register for that class online. There's something to do with that energy of registration that will kind of set things in motion for you. Ask the class to contribute to you. Once you've registered, you start being in the question all the time. Ask a question every single day. "What would it take for me to go to this class?" Write down a list of your expenses and you can ask, "What would it take to have this much money and more showing up right away?" Just be in the question and see what that creates. Also destroy and uncreate all your projections, expectations, separations, rejections, and judgments about having that. We all create something and then we have projections and expectations about it. These projections and expectations just kill it. So destroy and uncreate all your projections and expectations every single day.

Run your Hopes and Dreams Bar. (The Bars® are 32 bars of energy, which run through and around your head, storing the electromagnetic component of all the thoughts, ideas, attitudes, decisions and beliefs that you have ever had about anything. There are bars for Healing, Body, Control, Awareness, Creativity, Power, Aging, Sex and Money just to name a few. Each thought, idea, attitude, decision or belief that you have fixed in place solidifies the energy and limits your capacity to be generative in that area. The purpose of an Access Bars® session is to clear those points and to invite people to receive, receiving instead of doing, doing, doing.) So you let go of the expectations.

That's how you start creating money. Sometimes it takes time for the universe to gift you what you are asking for. The universe has to literally re-arrange itself to gift you what you are asking for.

Caller: Is there a clearing to get beyond being terrified of spending money on myself? I'm doing my best to pull energy. And, that's when all the other stuff shows up, like being selfish to put this kind of financial burden on my partner. I know it's unimportant, yet it's there. And I'm doing my best not to judge myself.

Nilofer: All the distractor implants of fear, of fear about money and everything underneath that, keeping that in place, will you destroy and uncreate it all? Right and Wrong, Good and Bad, POD, POC, All 9, Shorts, Boys and Beyonds®

What have you made so vital about the distractor implants of fear, doubt and worry about money that you would give up the true abundance you truly be? Everything that is times godzillion will you destroy and uncreate it all? Right and Wrong, Good and Bad, POD, POC, All 9, Shorts, Boys and Beyonds®

Every time you have this fear or worry about money coming up, run these clearings on yourself about distractor implants. Also, a good place to start is "Who does that belong to? Is it mine? Someone else? Something else?" Then just return it all back to sender with consciousness attached.

Caller: I had thought about all that I created and realized that many times I had the possibilities show up in relation to the question; and then it didn't actually materialize. For example I asked "What would it take to have the money show up to pay the mortgage this month?" And then I got a call for helping someone and they would pay the exact amount that I needed. And I said "Wow! Awesome! I'm good." And then the next day the logistics were too complicated, the travel and gas too expensive to make it worth my while. But I still decided to just do it, to send the universe positive action on my part. And then a day later, it won't happen. So that was just one example. So then – "What would it take to augment my income?" And I get a call from someone with a proposition. He sends me a contract to review or sign. I want a few changes for my benefit and reply. Later he has health issues and the deal falls through.

Nilofer: When you have the possibility show up, do you immediately go to this place of conclusion or do you go to a place of question? When we have a possibility about income show up, in our heads we immediately go this place of "I'll have this much money and this and this." So you've already done the project, got the money, spent it: all mentally. When you've done it mentally, most of the time it's not going to actualize in the physical reality. Instead, go to question. "How does it get any better than this?® What else is possible here?® What else does this require?" Just go to question.

The other thing that you also have to realize is that just because these couple of things fell through does not mean that the infinite universe is not gifting to you. It is an infinite universe. And you have infinite possibilities available to you all the time. So this is just a muscle. Practice it. You will have more and more and more possibilities showing up. And just go to the above question. Alternatively, you could also ask these four questions: "What is this? What can I do with it? Can I change it? And, if so, how can I change it?"

ENTITIES

Caller: After I did the exercise of lowering down the barriers more and more, what came to me is that I have an energy that keeps me from being able to get money. It's like I have some vows and I don't know, it's bigger. From that moment I keep hearing voices in my head, like "You can't do that." Of course, I do the clearings. Yet I have voices like "We have to do this." And it's always a "We". It's not a "me."

Nilofer: Truth: how many entities do you have in your body? When you hear voices in your head which go "You can't do this," then it's not actually you because we don't think as "you." We think as "I'd" like to do this, and "I'd" like to do that. So when you are hearing these voices which are going "you," then it means that you have other beings without bodies which are there in your body. If you would like to clear these beings ask, "Truth Entities, who are you? Who were you before that? Who were you before that? Who were you before that? Who were you before that? Truth: who will you be in the future? Pack your bags; take all your magnetic and chemical imprints. Go with consciousness attached." Right and Wrong, Good and Bad, POD, POC, All 9, Shorts, Boys and Beyonds®

Close your eyes for a moment. Do you have more space or less space? There's no right answer.

I was just so aware of the barriers going up and the barriers going down. What I'm also starting to have an awareness of is how much information and how much awareness we are receiving when we actually have our barriers down.

Be aware of your barriers when you are with people. I also have this awareness that at different times with the same person, I will have my barriers up and my barriers down. Just be really present to what's going on. "Do I have my barriers up or do I have my barriers down?" One really good indication of barriers up is when you are starting to feel uncomfortable. The moment you push your barriers down, you start to feel this ease in your universe. You start to experience this space and expansion in your universe. Sometimes you will still be aware of this energy of contraction, but somehow it will not impact you. Just make yourself aware of it. You have this awareness of it belonging to someone else or something else. And you can use that energy because it is free energy. You can use it to contribute to your life.

COOL INTERVIEWS!

To listen to cool interviews with Access Consciousness Facilitators, including Gary Douglas, visit http://www.moneycirclebook.com

---

CHAPTER THREE

WHAT IS YOUR MONEY STORY

"It's Your Choice, NOT Your STORY That Creates Your Reality."
~ Dr Dain Heer

All of us have a money story. This is just a story. It is not real. We live our life from this story, because we think it is real. We have bought into the lie that it is real. This story is all the points of view that we have bought about money and how our reality with money is.

Take a pen and a piece of paper. Write down, "My money story is…" Don't think too much about it. Write down whatever comes to your mind about your whole money situation. Don't edit it, make any changes or think too much about it. Just write down whatever comes to your mind.

Once you are done, read your money story. As you are reading your money story, you will perceive this energy which comes up. This energy is all the limitations, all the points of views and all the beliefs that you have about money. As you are reading it, say "Everything that is will you destroy and uncreate it times godzillion."

Destroy because you are destroying the limitation. Uncreate because you have created that story in the first place. So, you are the one who is going to uncreate it. And godzillion is a number so big that God alone knows what that number is. Then you will use this weird, wacky phrase from Access Consciousness®, which is called *The Clearing Statement*. This is like

Harry Potter's magic wand. The clearing statement zaps that energy out of existence. The Access Consciousness® Clearing Statement is "Right and Wrong, Good and Bad, POD, POC, All 9, Shorts, Boys and Beyonds®."

Read your story once again. Destroy and uncreate it using the clearing statement. Keep repeating this until you feel like there is no charge around the story. The next day, once again, write down your money story. You will find that you have written something totally different. Read it once again, and destroy and uncreate it until you have no charge around it whatsoever.

Do this every day for the next one week.

One of the things that I have noticed is I will look at things and say, "I don't have the money for this!" Then I say, "Oh, look at that. What an amazing conclusion I have? Everything that is destroy and uncreate it. Right and Wrong, Good and Bad, POD, POC, All 9, Shorts, Boys and Beyonds®"

Throughout the day, just be aware of where you are buying into the limitation of money and not looking at the possibility of money. If you see this universe, it's a totally abundant universe. "Ask and you shall receive" is one of the laws of the universe. We buy into the limitations of this reality, and we don't even ask for what we would like to create in our life.

Do this for a week. You will reach the deeper layers of your money story and clear them. What we are actually doing is opening up all those places where we have locked ourselves with all these points of view that we have about money. Once you start unlocking it, you have all that energy available.

What's the value of having no money? Everything that brings up will you destroy and uncreate it all? Right and Wrong, Good and Bad, POD, POC, All 9, Shorts, Boys and Beyonds®

Another clearing which may open things up is:

What do you love about having no money? Everything that brings up will you destroy and uncreate it all? Right and Wrong, Good and Bad, POD, POC, All 9, Shorts, Boys and Beyonds®

LIE OF DESERVING

Caller: My money issue is that I have created very little in my life. I do not know what question to ask to clear the lack of money in my life. Both my parents, while they were embodied on Earth, gave to my siblings. When they passed, I was so shocked to realize that they left me out. I was in my twenties when my father passed. He left everything to my sister and her children. And she was wealthy, anyway. I was a single mom with small children. Mother did the same. So how do I change the belief that I deserve and that the universe has my back really? It takes all my freaking energy to give myself -- to give myself permission to buy clothes for myself."

Nilofer: Be aware that it's just a story.

Everything that brings up will you destroy and uncreate it all? Right and Wrong, Good and Bad, POD, POC, All 9, Shorts, Boys and Beyonds®

The thing with stories is that they are not real. You think they are real, and you can't really see outside of it. Just keep POCing and PODing through it until your whole story is gone. Then look at actually creating more money in your life.

The other part is about deserving. Do you deserve to breathe or do you just breathe? Deserving is another lie that we buy into.

All the ways you have bought into the lie of deserving anything, will you destroy and uncreate it all? Right and Wrong, Good and Bad, POD,

POC, All 9, Shorts, Boys and Beyonds®

Keep reading your story. Everything that brings up, destroy and uncreate it all. Just read your story a hundred times, two hundred times, however many times are required and POC and POD your way out of it. Once your whole story is gone, you will start to get a freedom around money that you've never had possible. See what opens up for you.

AWARENESS

Caller: Can you talk about Awareness? How do we know what it is, and how to trust it or hear it? Thank you.

Nilofer: Everything that you misidentified and misapplied awareness or lack of awareness as, will you destroy and uncreate it all? Right and Wrong, Good and Bad, POD, POC, All 9, Shorts, Boys and Beyonds®

We are actually aware all the time. It's just that we interpret things in our own way. For example, every time you have a sensation or intensity in your body it is awareness. What we usually do is come to a conclusion, "Oh, I have a pain in my head" or "I have this in my back," things like that. The moment we do that, we solidify that awareness. Then we are not really able to look there. What if you were able to question the awareness? "What is this? What can I do with it? Can I change it? And how can I change it?" The other question to go is "What awareness am I having here that I'm not acknowledging?"

Run your Awareness Bar (The Bars are 32 points on the head which when lightly touched releases the electrical charge that holds all the considerations, thoughts, ideas, beliefs, decisions, emotions or attitudes you have ever stored or decided was important in any lifetime.) every single night. All the points of view that we have about what awareness is, what it consists of and how much we are not aware—once you start running your awareness bar—you'll start to delete all those points of view and all those points you are holding on to. You will actually start being present with the awareness, which you are actually receiving all the time.

Go into question. "If I choose this, what will my life be like in 5 years of time? If I don't choose this, what will my life be like in 5 years?"

If you get an expansive energy for any of the questions, it means you are tapping into a more expansive future for you. Everything that feels light to you is true for you. Everything that feels heavy to you is not actually true for you. You are always aware. You just may not perceive it as awareness.

What awareness are you having that you are not acknowledging, that if you were to acknowledge it would change your whole reality? Everything that doesn't allow you to perceive, know, be, and receive that would you destroy and uncreate it all? Right and Wrong, Good and Bad, POD, POC, All 9, Shorts, Boys and Beyonds®

Caller: I would like to get my Bars run, but not many people around here are willing to.

Nilofer: Do you realize how many conclusions are attached to "people not willing to run bars," etc. Everything that is would you destroy and uncreate it all? Right and Wrong, Good and Bad, POD, POC, All 9, Shorts, Boys and Beyonds®

How many of you are unwilling to ask for any contribution to your life? Are you asking for contribution from your body? Are you asking for contribution from your home? Contribution is the simultaneity of gifting and receiving. What happens when you are willing to ask for contribution is you are gifting contribution and you are receiving. Contribution kind of adds to your life.

Let's do an exercise here. "Body, what contribution can you be to my life, my living, my reality, my future and my money flow; and what contribution can I be to you?" Now, become aware of your home and everything inside your home. What contribution can my home be to me, my life, my living, my body, my money flows, my reality and my future; and what contribution can I be to it?

Now, become aware of your car. What contribution could it be to my body, my life, my living, my reality and my money flows; and what contribution can I be to you?

Now, become aware of your job, your career or your business. What contribution can I be to you; and what contribution can you be to my life, my reality, my future, my body and my money flows?

Now, become aware of Earth. What contribution can I be to you; and what contribution can you to be to me, my life, my living, my reality, my future, my body and my money flows?

Every molecule of the universe would like to actually gift to you when you are willing to ask for the contribution. You have to be willing to ask for that contribution.

DO YOU HAVE A MONEY CEILING?

Caller: I am making just enough to get by every month. It seems like I cannot go past the amount of what I am making right now. When I ask questions about making more than what I am making, for some reason I cannot believe that can happen. What else can I be or do different here that I am not aware? Thank you.

Nilofer: Do you have a money ceiling?

All the ceilings you have around money, from this lifetime or any other lifetime, will you now destroy and uncreate it all? Right and Wrong,

Good and Bad, POD, POC, All 9, Shorts, Boys and Beyonds®

This is a limit that you have placed on yourself, which you will not choose to go beyond. It's almost like the thermostat in an air-conditioner. When you set it at a particular temperature, the moment it goes above that it will come back to that temperature. The moment it goes below that, it will come back to that temperature.

How many ceilings do you have around money and money flows? Everything that is times godzillion will you destroy and uncreate it all? Right and Wrong, Good and Bad, POD, POC, All 9, Shorts, Boys and Beyonds®

The other thing I would ask: are you willing to be the richest person in your family? Everything that brought up or let down, will you destroy and uncreate it all? Right and Wrong, Good and Bad, POD, POC, All 9, Shorts, Boys and Beyonds®

What have you made so vital about possessing your family that you would not choose to create more money than them? Everything that is times godzillion will you destroy and uncreate it all? Right and Wrong, Good and Bad, POD, POC, All 9, Shorts, Boys and Beyonds®

Are you willing to have more money than your father? Everything that brings up, would you destroy and uncreate it all? Right and Wrong, Good and Bad, POD, POC, All 9, Shorts, Boys and Beyonds®

Are you willing to have more money than your mother? Everything that is times godzillion will you destroy and uncreate it all? Right and Wrong, Good and Bad, POD, POC, All 9, Shorts, Boys and Beyonds®

How many thoughts, feelings, emotions and points of view around money did you buy from your father before you were the age of 2? Everything that is times godzillion will you destroy and uncreate it all? Right and

Wrong, Good and Bad, POD, POC, All 9, Shorts, Boys and Beyonds®

How many thoughts, feelings, emotions and points of view around money did you buy from your mother before you were the age of 2? Everything that is times godzillion will you destroy and uncreate it all? Right and Wrong, Good and Bad, POD, POC, All 9, Shorts, Boys and Beyonds®

The other question that you can ask is "Who are you unwilling to have more money than?" Everything that brings up, will you destroy and uncreate it all? Right and Wrong, Good and Bad, POD, POC, All 9, Shorts, Boys and Beyonds®

Who are you willing to have more money than in your family? Everything that brings up or lets down, will you destroy and uncreate it all? Right and Wrong, Good and Bad, POD, POC, All 9, Shorts, Boys and Beyonds®

DEBTS

Caller: I owe my sister, my mother and my aunt about $20,000. My aunt is charging me her money now. And I feel very strange. At the same time I feel upset and offended for her charging me, even though it is her money. I am the one who takes care of the house with all the expenses and now this. What questions can I ask or what clearing can I do? Thank you.

Nilofer: Everything that brings up, will you destroy and uncreate it all? Right and Wrong, Good and Bad, POD, POC, All 9, Shorts, Boys and Beyonds®

This question is to do with past expenditure. Past expenditure is just the word that we use, because "debt" sounds very much like "death" D-E-A-T-H.

Look at how much you can actually take out and pay for your past expenditures every month. If you were to pay it off in one year's time, how much money would you have to pay every month? Or if you had to pay it off in two year's time, how much money would you have to pay every month? Then ask for that money to show up and start using it to pay off your past expenditure.

It's as simple as ask and you shall receive. Here's what you should do. Look at your expenses for a month. Now add the money that you will require to pay for your past expenditure. Then add some money which you can use to have some fun with. Then ask for that money to show up.

What would it take to have this amount of money show up every month? Or, what can I be or do different today to have this amount of money show up for me right away? Everything that doesn't allow it, destroy and uncreate it all. Right and Wrong, Good and Bad, POD, POC, All 9, Shorts, Boys and Beyonds®

One of the things that I have seen a lot of people do is that they will ask a question just once. What if you could keep asking the question all day? Once I wanted to create some money. So what I did was, as I lay down in my bed at night, I looked at my bank account. I looked at it and asked "What else is possible here?®" "What else is possible here?®" "What else is possible here?®" I must have asked that question over and over for 15-20 minutes. Money actually showed up in my bank account in the next 3-4 days.

If you have a money situation and you really would like to create money, ask "What else is possible here?" Continue asking, and POC and POD everything that doesn't allow it to show up. You have to demand, which doesn't mean demanding anything from the universe. It is about demanding from your own self. You are demanding yourself to be a different energy that will allow the thing that you are demanding to show up. Go "I don't care what it takes, I don't care what I have to be or do different, but I would like that money to show up right away."

I remember this little story. There was a Guru and he had a disciple. The disciple would go to the Guru asking him to teach him something. The Guru would never ever teach him anything. One day the disciple got really angry and said, "Why can't you teach me something? I have been coming to you for years and you haven't taught me anything. I would really like to be enlightened. You have to teach me something." The Guru said, "Ok, follow me." The Guru took the disciple outside to where a tank of water was located. The Guru called his disciple closer and plunged his disciple's neck into the water. The Guru kept holding his disciple's face without allowing his face to surface. The disciple, while struggling, thought "Oh my god, I'm going to die. I can't breathe. This is water!" The Guru finally released him. Then the Guru asked the disciple, "So how much did you want to breathe while you were inside the water? When you want enlightenment to the extent you wanted to breathe just now, you will get it."

A demand is when you have enough of all the things going on in your life, and you are like "I don't care what it takes, but this thing has to change right now." You have that need, like the disciple in the story had that need to breathe in water. When you be that demand, you will create it in your life.

Look at the question you are asking. Is it wishy-washy with all kinds of stuff in your mind? Are you being that demand to actually be able to breathe, and when you get there you will have it? How does it get any better than that?*

Caller: Could I have more clarity on past expenditures? Do we keep money aside every month for past expenditures? What do we do with this money we remove towards this?"

Nilofer: You can start paying off the past expenditure. Every month you decide the amount of money you would like to pay towards your past expenditure. Choose – would I like to pay this past expenditure in a year's time? Would I like to pay in 2 years time?

Based on your choice and the amount of your past expenditure, how much money would you be required to create every month? Then ask for that money to show up and start paying off your past expenditure. Then every month you are paying off that past expenditure. Soon you will be done with it.

CONFLICTUAL UNIVERSES WITH MONEY

Caller: I come from a really rich family. Yet, I can't ask for money from anybody for my therapy services. Why do I distribute all the money the moment I receive it? Why do I not want to handle the money and why do I want to leave this money?

Nilofer: The clearing you want to ask is "What do I hate about having money? Everything that is times godzillion will you destroy and uncreate it all? Right and Wrong, Good and Bad, POD, POC, All 9, Shorts, Boys and Beyonds®"

All the oaths, vows, swearings, bindings, bondings and contracts you have across all dimensions of time, space and reality about money, about never having money and about dirty money; will you now revoke, recant, renounce, denounce, destroy and uncreate it all? Right and Wrong, Good and Bad, POD, POC, All 9, Shorts, Boys and Beyonds®

You were born and live in a family that has a lot of money, yet you have a conflictual universe going on about not being able to charge for your therapy.

How many conflictual universes do you have about money that are stopping your money flows? Everything that is times godzillion will you destroy and uncreate it all? Right and Wrong, Good and Bad, POD, POC, All 9, Shorts, Boys and Beyonds®

Caller: I have two things together. Two feelings are: I am certain if I need money for something, I'll always get it. Second is: I cannot buy this now or have this now. Maybe I can in a few months or years when the money is there. Then something will happen, and I can have it. I practice Access tools, done many clearings. Conflictual reality is the one I am doing now.

Nilofer: All the conflictual universes you have created around money, will you destroy and uncreate it all? Right and Wrong, Good and Bad, POD, POC, All 9, Shorts, Boys and Beyonds®

CHARGING FOR YOUR SERVICES

Caller: Much is changing at speed. I'm finding that money is showing up in more places along with fun opportunities. That's great. How does it get any better than that?® My question relates to my business charging and time. I have quoted a new rate per hour. This particular rate is offering me joyful and fun gifts, and opportunities to expand. Using Access and other tools however, I find that I judge myself to be too slow because the hours are now building up or have concerns about the other person's expectations. I suspect this relates to projections, etc., making stuff vital. But no matter what clearings I have used, I am aware that there's heaviness here. The big thing is that after loads of clearings, etc., seeing myself resisting receiving to some degree.

Nilofer: Ask the work how much it would like to be charged. Ask "How much money would be fun for me?" You will get a figure. Often there's a distance between what you are charging and how much money would be fun for you.

You've asked "how much money would be fun for me to charge?" Then you can ask "What does charging this amount of money mean to me?" Everything that is times godzillion will you destroy and uncreate it all? Right and Wrong, Good and Bad, POD, POC, All 9, Shorts, Boys and Beyonds®

When you keep POCing and PODing that, all the points of view you have around charging that sum of money will start to disappear. Then you will start to create that money in your life.

Caller: One of the biggest "Ahas" about my money story was "money spoils kids or people", which then led me to realize that I bought the point of view that money spoils us and being spoiled is wrong or bad. So I came up with everything I perceived and everywhere I bought that point of view that being spoiled is wrong and bad, and therefore, cut out my receiving from the universe. So, now the question: I have a possibility for a corporate one-year project contract that feels light and aligned. I'm applying for this. At the same time I am noticing a too good to be true aspect, and will I be able to remain being me while being employed and not fall into this stress perceived in the corporate world? What clearing statements or energy can I be to receive this with ease?

Nilofer: Use this clearing: What does this corporate project mean to me? Everything that is times godzillion, destroy and uncreate it all. Right and Wrong, Good and Bad, POD, POC, All 9, Shorts, Boys and Beyonds®

Keep using this clearing 30 times a day for the next 30 days. See what changes and shifts for you. Then you could use this clearing: What have I made so vital about possessing this corporate project that I would give up all freedom, happiness and being me in order to have it? Everything that brings up, will I destroy and uncreate it all? Right and Wrong, Good and Bad, POD, POC, All 9, Shorts, Boys and Beyonds®

Another question you may want to use is "How does it get any better than this?®" Every time you have that awareness of this being too good to be true, go to question "How does it get any better than this?®" and "What else is possible here?®"

We sometimes actually forget to use the most basic tools Access Consciousness® teaches. So, go back to the tools of Access and use them.

ARE YOU AT THE EFFECT OF OTHER PEOPLE'S MONEY SITUATION?

Caller: How not to be at the effect of your life partner's money situation?

Nilofer: I love this question.

What creation are you using to invoke and perpetrate the biomimetic and biomimetric mimicry of other people's pain, pathways and reality around money are you choosing? Everything that is times godzillion will you destroy and uncreate it all? Right and Wrong, Good and Bad, POD, POC, All 9, Shorts, Boys and Beyonds®

The first thing you do is to run this clearing. You may want to run it 30 times a day for the next 30 or 90 days.

The other thing is to be aware that *you* are the creative source of *your* universe. Your life partner is not. What this basically means is if you are not working and your life partner is, then you start to buy into the lie that he is the source of your money and your income. That's not true. You can create money. You can create whatever money that you require.

Two other questions that I would gift you are "If I were being me today, what would I create right away?" and "What can I be or do different today to have my own reality around money right away?"

Be in the question, "What is my reality around money?" You may find that your reality around money is that you would like to have huge amounts of money, whereas your partner is not willing to have that amount of money. What if you could be in allowance of his willingness to have whatever amount of money he has? At the same time, you create the amount of money that you would like in your life. As you do the biomimetric mimicry clearing, you will start to disconnect from his monetary reality and start to create your own money reality.

Caller: Whenever I choose to change things around money, regardless of what it is I'm choosing, less shows up or stuff happens. For example, things breakdown, more bills show up, people don't pay me for my services, etc. It is like the opposite happens. What is that? Can you speak about that please? And it feels better not to change and stay with very limited money rather than have less show up or more problems arise.

Nilofer: When you start to do clearings about money, you are hitting deeper layers of your stuff. When you are saying that, it becomes worse, you are saying that there is change happening there. What if you were not to judge that change? What if you were to acknowledge, "I've been doing this clearing and this is the change which has showed up. How does it get any better than that?® Let me go for more clearings. Let me do more stuff. And, what else is possible here?®"

Everywhere you're judging change as good or bad, will you destroy and uncreate it all? Right and Wrong, Good and Bad, POD, POC, All 9, Shorts, Boys and Beyonds®

All the points of view you have about the way change is showing up, will you destroy and uncreate it all? Right and Wrong, Good and Bad, POD, POC, All 9, Shorts, Boys and Beyonds®

Most people say "Change has to happen in this way and this way and this way" rather than saying "I don't care what it takes, but I am changing everything in my life. I don't care what it takes. I don't care what I have to give up and against who I have to lose. I don't care what I have to be or do different. Everything, everything in my life is changing now." When you be the demand, change will show up. Don't judge the change. Just keep asking for more and more. The problem is the moment you judge; you stop your receiving at that moment.

WHAT ELSE IS POSSIBLE HERE?

Caller: Sometimes I am not even able to remember one clearing statement. Get really frustrated with myself, especially when I get triggered. It's like all my molecules and neurons go haywire and shut down."

Nilofer: Everything that is times godzillion, will you destroy and uncreate it all? Right and Wrong, Good and Bad, POD, POC, All 9, Shorts, Boys and Beyonds®

What if you didn't have to remember anything? What if you could just use any tool? It could be a little question like "What else is possible here?®" Just keep using the question. It doesn't matter. Use a tool, any tool you can remember. Just play with it. When you are experiencing this, the molecules shut down and going haywire, what if you didn't make it wrong? What if you ask "What's right about this I'm not getting?" and "What awareness am I having here?"

JUDGMENT

Caller: "How does one get out of the cesspool without judgment?"

Nilofer: Just look at where you are at and say "Wow! I am such an amazing creator! I've created this huge cesspool. What an amazing capacity for creation I have here! How does it get any better than that?®"

Are you aware that that's a capacity you have for creation? "I am such a potent creator of magnitude. Thank you universe for helping me create this. What would it take for us to have something different show up?" If you can laugh at this cesspool in your life and get that you are a creator of magnitude to be able to create that, then where else can you use those creative capacities to create?

All the cesspools in your life that you are making really significant, will you destroy and uncreate it all? Right and Wrong, Good and Bad, POD, POC, All 9, Shorts, Boys and Beyonds®.

What creative capacities for creating cesspools do you have that you are not acknowledging that if you were to acknowledge it, you could use it to create more money than God? Everything that is times godzillion will you destroy and uncreate it all? Right and Wrong, Good and Bad, POD, POC, All 9, Shorts, Boys and Beyonds®

Get that energy of the cesspool. Then get that creative capacity which has created that cesspool. Then use that energy to create whatever you would like to in life. It's just free energy. When you are labeling it as a cesspool, that's when you go "I can't use this, it's horrible!" Yet if you have no label around it, it's just energy. Find the parts of your life where you can contribute that free energy to.

CAN I HAVE THE MONEY NOW PLEASE?

Caller: I have been asking questions for money to show up now and have only been seeing money come in change or a few dollars. Also having resistance to asking for money for the clearing circle I run each week. How can I get paid for using my gifts and doing what I love?

Caller: I've been offering my work for free, for practice and gifts, for a few weeks. But now I don't feel like doing this work anymore. And

I'm resentful for the immediate result people are receiving, without me receiving any payment. How can I change?

(These are 2 questions which address the same energy)
Nilofer: Is it working for you to do it free for people now? Clearly it isn't. So you have to start charging for your work. Just practice asking "Can I have the money now please?" Just ask. Ask for the money from the clearing circle you are running. Ask for people to pay up. There will be some who will pay and come. There will be some who will not pay and not come. If you don't have a point of view about this, just ask for the money to show up.

How much you are holding on to your story around money and how much are you making it significant? POC and POD all your points of view about your money story. Then that entire story starts to disappear from your universe. You will have a level of freedom with money and with creating money that you have never ever had in your life before.

What have you made so vital about possessing your money story that you would give up all receiving in order to have it? Everything that is times godzillion will you destroy and uncreate it all? Right and Wrong, Good and Bad, POD, POC, All 9, Shorts, Boys and Beyonds®

What have you made so vital about possessing no money that you would give up having it? Everything that is times godzillion will you destroy and uncreate it all? Right and Wrong, Good and Bad, POD, POC, All 9, Shorts, Boys and Beyonds®

What energy, space and consciousness can your body and you be to have never enough money and more money than you can ever spend? Everything that doesn't allow you to perceive, know, be and receive that, will you destroy and uncreate it all? Right and Wrong, Good and Bad, POD, POC, All 9, Shorts, Boys and Beyonds®

Caller: So when you ask the question "Can I have the money now please?" do you actually ask that of people who owe you money for your goods? What do you do if they don't pay then? What else can you do if they ignore your request to pay you the money and their account is overdue? It makes me really angry and frustrated that they don't want to pay you and don't value your service, etc.?

Nilofer: Ask the question from people who owe you money. Practice it in front of the mirror every day. Then start asking for money to show up.

There was a woman who had to pay me money for some classes that she had taken with me. She had not paid me for a year. I sent a text to her, "You have to pay me this much money for a class you took one year ago and can I have the money now please?"

You **have** to be in that energy of "Can I have the money now please? You have to pay me."

You **have** to be that energy. I was being that energy when I sent her that text. Immediately I got a response from her, "I'm so sorry. I will pay you in a couple of days' time." She did not pay me after 2 days. I could have thought, "I've already asked her and she has not paid me again." Instead, I asked her again. "Can I have the money now please? It's two days now and you have to pay me." I kept following up with her until eventually she actually paid me.

Just get over your points of view. When you have a point of view about being angry and frustrated when people are not paying you, how much are you being that invitation for receiving that money? You are not.

Here's what you do. You start pulling energy from people who owe you money. Start pulling energy from behind them, through them, to you and then send out trickles of energy back to that person. Do it every day. Ask the energy to run all day long. They will not be able to get you out of their mind at all. Do that, and ask "Can I have the money now please?" with that energy of "You better pay me now! I've had enough of this!" When you can do that, you will start seeing the money coming in. If the money comes in, that's great. If it doesn't, never mind.

THE JOY OF BEING A NOT DOCTOR

Would you like to change the incurable in your body? Pain, illness or body image insecurities? Listen to the interview with Liam Philips and Bret Rushia http://www.moneycirclebook.com

CHAPTER FOUR

LET'S TALK ABOUT MAGIC

"That's the thing with magic. You've got to know it's still here, all around us, or it just stays invisible for you."
~ Charles de Lint

How much in your life do you create from magic? Magic is everyday magic. When things happen unexpectedly in your life, which would not have happened, that is magic. When you ask for things to show up and they show up, that's magic. As infinite beings we actually create from magic and from energy.

We are going to tap into the magic. We are going to tap into the energy that we already are to actually create. We can create anything we desire in our life. We can create money, we can create wealth, we can create riches, and we can create possibilities.

What energy, space and consciousness can your body and you be to be the magic, the wizardry, the witchcraft and the sorcery you truly be for all eternity? Everything that doesn't allow that, destroy and uncreate it all times godzillion. Right and Wrong, Good and Bad, POD, POC, All 9, Shorts, Boys and Beyonds®

Repeat the above clearing 30 times a day for the next 30 days.

As you do this, start to notice what kind of magic shows up in your life.

What stupidity are you using to avoid the magic, the wizardry, the witchcraft and the sorcery that you could be choosing are you choosing? Everything that is times godzillion will you destroy and uncreate it all? Right and Wrong, Good and Bad, POD, POC, All 9, Shorts, Boys and Beyonds®

What physical actualization of the magic, the wizardry, the witchcraft and the sorcery are you now capable of generating, creating and instituting? Everything that doesn't allow that, will you destroy and uncreate it all? Right and Wrong, Good and Bad, POD, POC, All 9, Shorts, Boys and Beyonds®

Caller: I've been hearing from people how money is showing up for them unexpectedly and I am wondering "How does it get any better than this?® and What else is possible here?®"

Nilofer: Just lower your barriers and now expand out. Expand to the space of one hundred thousand miles in all directions and down into Earth. Keep expanding beyond that and tap into energy of magic, sorcery, wizardry and witchcraft. Start pulling that energy from all over the universe. Pull it into your body and beyond. Keep pulling and exponentialise that energy. Step it up.

Now tap into your capacities, talents and abilities with magic, wizardry, witchcraft and sorcery across all schematics of time, space and reality. Everything that doesn't allow you to perceive, know, be and receive that, destroy and uncreate it all. Right and Wrong, Good and Bad, POD, POC, All 9, Shorts, Boys and Beyonds®

What if everything that you created came from this energy of magic? What if you were to acknowledge it? What if you were to actually ask for its contribution in creating everything in your life, including your money flows?

It's great to use this clearing. You will have money showing as if by magic in your life. What if you could actually start creating the money? What can you add to your life today to create money for you and your living right away? Be in the question and you just start creating things. What if you could use this energy of magic, wizardry, witchcraft and sorcery to create everything?

ARE YOU TRYING TO GET IT RIGHT?

Caller: Two years ago I used to have many clients. I would sell packages to them. Then I started teaching classes. Now I don't have many sessions. Even my classes are too small or sometimes nobody comes. I know in Access we say "be the energy" but I also know that I do nothing to go out and promote myself. What can I ask or do here please?

Okay and my other question is that I feel like I am required to do something bigger now, like video or teleclasses. Then I go into judgement that I don't know technology. What can I be or do here? Thank you.

Nilofer: Let's look at the first part of the question. Tap into the energy of when you were having clients and when you sold many packages. What were you being or doing different then than what you do now? Everything that doesn't allow you to perceive, know, be and receive that, will you destroy and uncreate it all? Right and Wrong, Good and Bad, POD, POC, All 9, Shorts, Boys and Beyonds®

Just lower your barriers and get the energy of 2 years ago when you had a lot of clients and when you were selling packages. Ask that energy to contribute to your business, to your classes, to your sessions and to your money flows right now, today and in the future. Can you perceive how that energy expands as it contributes to your life? Use that energy to contribute to some other area of your life. What else would you like to create? What about asking for its contribution to creating videos or tele-classes or anything else that you would like to do? What else would you like to create today? What about asking that energy to contribute energy to all of your creations? Notice that every time you ask for that energy to contribute to anything, it keeps expanding and expanding. What else can you ask that energy to contribute to? Would you like to contribute to Earth or to creating a different reality in your relationship? There's all this free energy in the universe. Once you start asking for the contribution from this energy, it just starts expanding. You could just use it anywhere and everywhere.

Most people go into this place of "I have to get this right. I have to get this good. I have to get this perfect." Everything that is will you destroy and uncreate it all? Right and Wrong, Good and Bad, POD, POC, All 9, Shorts, Boys and Beyonds®

Instead of "I feel I'm required to do something bigger," ask "Business, what else do you require of me? What else can I create here that I haven't even considered?" If technology pops into your awareness, ask "If I choose this, what will my life be like in 5 years time? If I don't choose this, what will my life be like in 5 years time?" and "If I create this, what will the earth be like in 50 years time, in 100 years time?" Be the question and then ask "In how many ways can I do this wrong?" and "How much fun can I have in doing this wrong?" When you are actually giving yourself permission to be wrong, to actually fail at something, you just have this freedom to do it in whatever way you want. What does it matter if you get it wrong or if you fall flat on your face? Just lift yourself up, dust yourself off and carry on. Just have fun creating it. Don't go into the rightness or wrongness of it. If you are going into it, POC and POD all of that.

RELATIONSHIPS AND MONEY

Caller: "When I have problems with my boyfriend at home or we argue, I am very aware that my money stops. What can I do here?"

Nilofer: Be that place where money follows joy. As long as you are having fun, you will have the money. When you are not having fun, you have issues show up in your relationship and in your money flows.

When that happens, POC and POD all your issues. Get over it. Change your situation. Ask these questions: What can I be or do different today to change this right away? What question can I ask here to change this? What choices do I have here? What possibilities are available here that I haven't yet acknowledged? And, what contribution can I be or receive here?

When you create that change in your relationship, you'll find the money flows start to show up. Mostly when you are creating an area in your life and everything is starting to fall in place, it's almost like you create this self-sabotage. You will create an issue in some other area of your life, just so you will not step into the potency of the creation that you are doing. Just kind of breakthrough to the next level. When that happens, be aware of it and POC and POD all that.

What have you made so vital about possessing your trauma-drama with your boyfriend that you would stop all your money flows in order to have it? Everything that is times godzillion will you destroy and uncreate it all? Right and Wrong, Good and Bad, POD, POC, All 9, Shorts, Boys and Beyonds®

Caller: Thank you for this awesome series. What a gift of awesome contribution to me it is! Income increased by at least $3,000 per month so far! And gifted $1,500. How does it get any better than that?® What else is possible?® Yeah! Woo-hoo! And what would it take for more of that to show up? And what would it take for me to out-create that 1,000-fold today?

I am aware of money stories. Then I uncreate and destroy all other stories beneath that. Then I get all confused and dizzy, and it doesn't seem to change beyond that. What questions or processes will help me change this now? I just keep asking, "Who does this belong to? And what will change that?"

Nilofer: What have you made so vital about possessing your money stories that you would cut off all receiving in order to have that? Everything that is will you destroy and uncreate it all? Right and Wrong, Good and Bad, POD, POC, All 9, Shorts, Boys and Beyonds®

Keep running this process and see what changes for you. Sometimes, when you get to that place of confusion and dizzy, it might be that your body requires sugar, salt, water or energy. And you are just vortexing? (Vortexing is when you touch into that oneness, that god-source, whatever you want to call it, that you actually are. When that occurs, there is no charge in your universe that can be dealt with. The charge goes away and the electrical component ceases to exist.)

Just relax for some time. You can use a clearing like, "What energy, space and consciousness can my body and I be to have never enough money and have more money than I can ever spend for all eternity? Everything that is times godzillion will I destroy and uncreate it all? Right and Wrong, Good and Bad, POD, POC, All 9, Shorts, Boys and Beyonds®"

Running this a few times will kind of shift and change something for you.

BEING

Caller: I'm having a hard time not doing and just being. How can I just be to have money? Can you explain a little bit more of that?

Nilofer: Most people think that just "being" means not doing anything. It's not that. When you're just being, you actually do everything. It's almost like you have this inspiration. You have this phenomenal energy which is guiding you to do this, to do that. Having your "being" is guiding what you do. When you are doing things from "being", it creates way more in your universe because you are totally present. You are totally aware. You have everything. You have all awareness. You don't have any judgments, so you are receiving everything at that point of time. Remember "being" is not actually the lack of doing, but "being" encompasses the fullness of doing.

PAYING FOR SESSIONS

Caller: I can charge for my sessions, but I have a hard time paying for a session. For me with this story, I don't have the money to buy it. And then I feel guilt for how people are going to do the same to me. Now, what can I do or ask in this situation? Thank you.

Nilofer: Everywhere you are lumping these two together, will you destroy and uncreate it all? Right and Wrong, Good and Bad, POD, POC, All 9, Shorts, Boys and Beyonds®

"If money wasn't the issue, what would you choose?" Often when you be in that question, you will then get to the real choice instead of making money the exchange commodity of your choice.

Once you get to the real choice, you can also ask "If I choose this, what will my life be like in 5 years time? If I don't choose this, what will my life be like in 5 years time?" Then follow the energy. There have been many times when I actually had that thing going on with money and I wanted to receive sessions. So I just asked the question "If I choose this, what will my life be like in 5 years time?" In some cases if I got that it was more expansive if I choose this, I did it regardless. What I found was that it increased and expanded my life in ways which was just phenomenal.

Also, there was a lot of money coming in. If you get that not choosing it is going to make your life expansive, make that choice.

WEIGHT

Caller: Right now when you talk about being, I was aware that I got about 50 pounds more since I've been doing healing work and Access Consciousness®. My boyfriend and I moved in together, and I stopped dancing. I love dancing. He does not dance. So I wonder what you could suggest here. Thank you.

Nilofer: When we are in a relationship, most of us give up pieces and parts of us to fit in the expectations that we have of the expectations our partner has. It's like almost like we divorce pieces and parts of us.

What if you were to start dancing again? What if it was okay for you to start dancing again even if he does not dance? What choice do you have here? It's actually a choice to just stop dancing or start dancing again. What if you were to do all the things that you love to do and just choose to do it. It is just a choice. Just do it.

About the 50 pounds overweight that you got since you started doing healing work and Access Consciousness®. How much more aware are you now? Are you aware of all the people who are overweight? I wonder if your body is pulling out the weight from other people.

When you become more aware, you are aware of other people's issues and you kind of fix it in your body. Ask "Who does this belong to?®" Then return it all back to sender with consciousness attached. You can also use this clearing: "What creation are you using to invoke and perpetrate the biomimetic and biomimetric mimicry of other people's pain, pathways and realities with body and weight are you choosing? Everything that is times godzillion will you destroy and uncreate it all? Right and Wrong, Good and Bad, POD, POC, All 9, Shorts, Boys and Beyonds®"

Run this clearing 30 times a day for the next 30 days. Notice what changes in your body as a result of running this clearing.

RECEIVING JUDGMENTS

Caller: I'd like to know what you do to allow yourself to receive judgments. How do you handle it when someone starts judging you?

Nilofer: Lower your barriers. That's the way you receive everything, including judgments. Think about the person who is judging you right now. Think about somebody who has judged you in the past and their judgments. Put your barriers up and see what that feels like. Then put the barriers down. See what happens to that judgment.

This is one of the most phenomenal ways in which you can receive judgments. Remember, every time that you do receive judgment, you have $5,000 into your bank account at the end of the year. How does it get any better than that?

What energy, space and consciousness can your body and you be to receive all judgments with total ease for all eternity? Everything that doesn't allow it times godzillion will you destroy and uncreate it all? Right and Wrong, Good and Bad, POD, POC, All 9, Shorts, Boys and Beyonds®

Caller: If I had a lot of money, I wouldn't want to tell my family. It would really change my whole life having that much money. I don't want to tell people and especially my spouse. I wouldn't be allowed to do what I would want to do with the money. Otherwise it would impact my relationship.

Nilofer: How aware are you of how much people are going to judge you for having that money when it comes in? If it works for you, just for fun, never tell anyone.

About allowance, use the following clearing: "What have you made so vital about your relationship, about possessing your relationship that you would give up your freedom, your happiness and being you in order to have it? Everything that is times godzillion will you destroy and uncreate it all? Right and Wrong, Good and Bad, POD, POC, All 9, Shorts, Boys and Beyonds®"

Run this process 30 times a day for the next 30 days. Notice how it starts unsticking you from that.

We go to these insane places in our relationships and cut off so much receiving, because we have cut ourselves off there, you know? This is an amazing clearing, which I have been actually running for the last few days. It has really helped open up a lot. You could put in the name of your boyfriend or husband asking, "what have I made so vital about so-and-so's name, relationship and marriage that I would give up freedom, happiness, money flows and being me in order to have it?"

If you can, be in the questions, "What if I had too much money?" or "What does having too much money mean to me?" or "What does having more money than my family mean to me?" When you start asking these questions, you will start to become aware of all the insane points of view that you actually have around this and all the conclusions and points of view, which are actually stopping you from having money.

MORE MAGIC AND POSSIBILITIES WITH 990%

Play with the magic. Play with being 990% of you. Every day I begin my day with these clearings of magic and 990%. I do it 10-20 times and my whole day is different. My whole day is magical. I actually get a sense of being more of me when that happens. Play with it and see what else shows up for you.

What stupidity are you using to avoid being the 990% of you that you could be choosing are you choosing? Everything that is times godzillion will you destroy and uncreate it all? Right and Wrong, Good and Bad, POD, POC, All 9, Shorts, Boys and Beyonds®

What contribution is being the 990% to your life, your living, your body and your reality? Everything that is times godzillion will you destroy and uncreate it all? Right and Wrong, Good and Bad, POD, POC, All 9, Shorts, Boys and Beyonds®

What contribution is not being the 990% to your life, your living, your body and your reality? Everything that is times godzillion will you destroy and uncreate it all? Right and Wrong, Good and Bad, POD, POC, All 9, Shorts, Boys and Beyonds®

The reason I'm running this 990% is because when you start being 990%, you are that place of having more of you. You are choosing to create the magic and everything else in your life.

What stupidity are you using to create the absolute and total lack of being the 990% are you choosing? Everything that is times godzillion will you destroy and uncreate it all? Right and Wrong, Good and Bad, POD, POC, All 9, Shorts, Boys and Beyonds®

You have to be willing to become more than you already are. So when you become willing to be 990%, then you become willing to be everything. How many times have you heard that "Be 100% that you are?" That kind of always used to stick me. What if you could be 1,000%? When you are willing to be 1,000%, you can then choose to be 990%. Because then you cannot define, you cannot limit it and the unknown, the unexplored and the uncomfortable are the beginning of awareness. When you start functioning from the unknown, the uncomfortable, and the unexplored; you can be in the question "What possibility am I aware of that I am not choosing?"

Right now we all are kind of choosing to be 10%. I wonder what you would create in your life if you were starting to choose the 990%.

What have you made so vital to avoid possessing the 990% that you would give up being the phenomenal you in order to have it? Everything that is times godzillion will you destroy and uncreate it all? Right and Wrong, Good and Bad, POD, POC, All 9, Shorts, Boys and Beyonds®

What have you made so vital about possessing the lack of 990% that you would give up being the phenomenal you in order to have it? Everything that is times godzillion will you destroy and uncreate it all? Right and Wrong, Good and Bad, POD, POC, All 9, Shorts, Boys and Beyonds®

What physical actualization of being the 990% of what you truly be are you now capable of generating, creating and instituting? Everything that doesn't allow that to show up times godzillion, will you destroy and uncreate it all? Right and Wrong, Good and Bad, POD, POC, All 9, Shorts, Boys and Beyonds®

What physical actualization of being the totality of 990% you truly be are you now capable of generating, creating and instituting? Everything that is times godzillion will you destroy and uncreate it all? Right and Wrong, Good and Bad, POD, POC, All 9, Shorts, Boys and Beyonds®

Play with these clearings of magic. Play with the energy of 990%. Play with the clearings of magic, wizardry, witchcraft and sorcery. Notice what starts to shift and change. As you become more and more of who you are, you also become more magnetic to money, wealth and riches showing up in your life.

What would happen if you had too much money? Everything that brings up or lets down, will you destroy and uncreate it all? Right and Wrong, Good and Bad, POD, POC, All 9, Shorts, Boys and Beyonds®

What would happen if you had way too much money? Everything that is times godzillion will you destroy and uncreate it all? Right and Wrong, Good and Bad, POD, POC, All 9, Shorts, Boys and Beyonds®

What choice could you make now that would allow more money into your life? Everything that doesn't allow it would you destroy and uncreate it all? Right and Wrong, Good and Bad, POD, POC, All 9, Shorts, Boys and Beyonds®

Would you be willing to be the richest person in your family that every-body came to get money from? The reason you don't want money is that you don't want to have to say "no" to those who need it when they come to you. This is totally insane. Everything that brings up or lets down, will you destroy and uncreate it all? Right and Wrong, Good and Bad, POD, POC, All 9, Shorts, Boys and Beyonds®

What physical actualization of a $100 million are you now capable of generating, creating and instituting? Everything that doesn't allow that to show up times godzillion will you destroy and uncreate it all? Right and Wrong, Good and Bad, POD, POC, All 9, Shorts, Boys and Beyonds®

What space can you be that would allow you to be the ease, speed and magic you truly be? Be in the question and have fun.

DOING THINGS DIFFERENT

When you are confronted with, "*Wow this feels really big or this feels like a stretch*, instead of saying to yourself, "I can't do it," what if you ask, "How can I?" Listen in to see what each of the speakers does different, as I interview top Access Consciousness® Facilitators from around the world! http://www.moneycirclebook.com

---

CHAPTER FIVE

CREATING YOUR OWN REALITY

"What would you like to create your life as?"

In the past 2 years, I have been creating a lot in my life. Only recently I have started to get a sense of what is my own reality. We live our life in this reality which everybody else has created. What I have been looking at is, what is my own reality of things. What is my own reality with money? What is my own reality with business? What is my own reality with relationships? What is my own reality with my body? What I have started to get a sense of is that my reality is very different from this reality. We spend our whole life trying to be a part of this reality or trying to fit in this reality, instead of starting to look for what our reality is and asking for that to show up.

What is your reality?

One of the things I started doing about 2 years back is asking this question, "What would I like to create my life as?" Asking this question every single day and teaching it to everyone I have met since that day; what I started to notice was things started to show up in my life which I would never ever have imagined would be a part of my life. They just didn't exist in my thoughts about what my future would be like. The funny part is that once those things actually showed up, I just loved them! The energy was amazing! It was like things that I didn't even know I was looking for would show up, and they were exactly what I required at that time. That's the kind of magic that started to show up in my life. Now when I look at it, what I am really aware of is that asking this question was the beginning of my own reality showing up.

I started asking that question about my relationship, "What would I like to create my relationship as?" What started to show up was fun, joy and adventure. I started to go out on dates with my husband. We would go to these little cafes. We would sit there with each other and just giggle like little teenagers, you know? We started going out for these adventure trips, which our whole family loves. Before that my relationship was so serious! That was the beginning of me asking for my reality with relationships.

I also started asking this question "What would I like to create my life as?" One of the things that showed up was I got my own TV show, *The Nilofer Show*, on a Hindi channel in India. I almost fell off my chair when I first got that offer. I thought, "Really! They want me to host a TV show?" I had never even considered a TV show. I was a telesummit host, and I loved interviewing people on an audio medium. I loved being on that TV show! I just enjoyed it. It was so much fun. I was treated like a star, and I loved it!

Start asking this question every single day, "What would I like to create my life as?"

"What would I like to create my money flows as?"

"What would I like to create my business as?"

"What would I like to create my body as?"

"What would I like to create my relationship as?"

"What would I like to create my job as?"

The other question, which you can also use, is, "If I were choosing for me today, what would I create?" You can also ask "What is my reality with money?" Being in these questions every single day will allow your reality to show up.

Your reality is way beyond this reality. What is your reality with money? Is it having lots of money? Is it having, luxuries, opulence and decadence? Is it travelling business class? Whatever it is, start asking it to show up.

One of the things I have been really exploring in the last few weeks has been creating my own reality. Your own reality is not part of this reality. It is a totally different reality. It's what is true for you, and it is a reality that actually works for you. I started to get a glimpse of this when I first came to Access Consciousness® about two and a half years ago. I started asking this question "What would I like to create my life as?"

Just being in that question started opening up so many things for me. Things would actualize in my universe. I would look at them and think "Wow! I didn't even know that this was what I wanted!" It's quite amazing to see all of that happening. I've been getting glimpses of my own reality for the last two and a half years, and I will remain in that of creating my own reality.

There will be times when I will just slip out of that, just slide out of that reality. That's when things start to get difficult and things go wrong in my universe. What if you were to start creating your own reality? Not just about money, but what if you were to create your own reality about life? The kind that extended into every aspect of your life: into your relationship, into your money flows, into your job or career, and into your body.

Ask "What would I like to create my reality as?" Get the energy of this. This energy feels light and expansive. Start pulling energy from all over the universe into that energy. Keep pulling energy and then send back trickles of energy to all people all over the universe looking for you and don't even know it. Ask the energy to equalize when the people find you. Do this every day. What would it be like if you were to start creating your life like that every single day?

MY MONEY COMES THROUGH OTHER PEOPLE

Caller: Hi. I always get what I really ask for, but through other people. It is very rare that I am the source of income. It's a blessing I guess, but it makes me feel dependent and that doesn't allow me to enjoy it. How do I change all this into more fun? I earn rarely but whenever I do, I don't get to use it. That is so annoying. How do I change this? I'm really amazing in everything I do, but I don't get the ground to play with my awesomeness. Please help me with this.

Nilofer: How many points of view do you have about this thing? When you are saying that "I find it makes me feel dependent," you are cutting off your receiving. Everything that doesn't allow you to receive everything that is coming to you, will you destroy and uncreate it all? Right and Wrong, Good and Bad, POD, POC, All 9, Shorts, Boys and Beyonds®

The other thing is you have to start is running this clearing: "What can I add to my life today to create more money flows right away? Everything that doesn't allow it, destroy and uncreate it all. Right and Wrong, Good and Bad, POD, POC, All 9, Shorts, Boys and Beyonds®"

When you are creating your life, you have to be in the question every single day. Do the energy flows. When something shows up in your life that matches the energy, take action on it. It's a very important creation component to take action when things are showing up in your life. You can POC and POD the things that come. You can do everything for it to come. Yet, unless you actually go out and take action, things are not going to move for you.

You are awesome. I get that you are awesome. Just be with the question, "How can I play with my awesomeness today?" Everything that doesn't allow it, destroy and uncreate it all. Right and Wrong, Good and Bad, POD, POC, All 9, Shorts, Boys and Beyonds®

WHEN THINGS ARE NOT CHANGING

Caller: I have been following your Money Circle videos but haven't noticed much improvement in my money. As you mentioned, what kind of things you can do to bring you joy and if you were to do one of them every day would bring you more money. My answer was running Bars. So last week, a friend called me to her place to run her Bars (The Bars are 32 points on the head which when lightly touched releases the electrical charge that holds all the considerations, thoughts, ideas, beliefs, decisions, emotions or attitudes you have ever stored or decided was important in any lifetime.) and later she mentioned that she will pay me later. This really disappointed me. I would love to know why there is lack of money flow. What else can I do to get the money I desire?

Nilofer: You are asking to create your own reality with money. You are in question. You are asking. You are using the tools of Access Consciousness®, and then, you judge it. You put a time frame to it and go into the judgment that this is not working for you. When you go into judgment, you actually will change everything there. So nothing is actually going to be available to you because you are going into the judgment of this.

All the projections, expectations, separations, rejections and judgments you have about the money circle, about how money has to show up in your life, about you, about me, and about anything else that will stop your receiving, will you destroy and uncreate it all? Right and Wrong, Good and Bad, POD, POC, All 9, Shorts, Boys and Beyonds®

The moment you go into judgment, you are killing the energy. It's almost like you remain one step away from actualizing whatever has to show up in your life and then you going into judgment will kill the energy. What if you were to go, "Wow! I created this and how does it get any better than this? What else is possible here that I haven't even considered?" With this, just go into question and it can be any question here.

"What can I be or do different today to change my money situation right away?"

The other thing with being in the question is about how I be in question all the time. So I will be continuously in the question all day and all night. Sometimes, if I am looking to change a particular situation, I will literally chant the question like a mantra. Sometimes it requires asking the question for 15 minutes to receive the solution. Sometimes you may have to do it for 15 days for things to change for you.

What if you did not allow your judgment, that projection to solidify you, and just continued to be in the question?

Somebody asked me to do a session for their mother. I went to their house. I did the session and for some reason, I was not able to ask for the money. I walked out of the house and said to myself "That was so amazing. I refused that for what reason? What would it take for me to change that?"

Go to question again. If you make yourself wrong, make the other person wrong or if you make anything else wrong, you are never ever going to change it. Yet if you go to question, if you acknowledge what is and be in allowance of you for whatever you have chosen, then ask for something else to show up, that's when something else will show up.

"Ask and you shall receive." It's as simple as that.

My favorite question is, "What would it take for XYZ to show up/actualize?" I use this for everything. I use it for creating things. I use this for learning skills. I use it to change my point of view, as well. Sometimes I look at myself and I think "I'm choosing that point of view, it's so heavy. I find it difficult to change this. What would it take for me to change that?" Things just change!

It can be as easy as "ask and you shall receive?" Play with it and see what shows up for you from there.

DRUGS AND MONEY

Caller: I have a boyfriend who has money or makes money, and he is going to spend it all on drugs. He has done it in the past. He has changed so much and is not doing them right now. I have done so much work on me on not stopping him doing it and letting him be, but I am aware that I do not want to be with him or even like him. I hate him when he does drugs. Also I'm aware I'm cutting my receiving from him. What can I be or do different here? Thank you for your contribution.

Nilofer: Here's the thing, what if you were to not judge you for anything including judgment?

Everywhere you are judging you, will you destroy and uncreate it all? Right and Wrong, Good and Bad, POD, POC, All 9, Shorts, Boys and Beyonds®

When you say that he has worked on himself and he has changed, you've come to a conclusion. You will cut off your receiving and awareness when you come to a conclusion about that.

Truth: has he changed? Yes, for the moment he has changed. Truth: does he have the capacity to do drugs again? Yes. Will he choose to do it? You have to be in question and be in question about everything.

Be aware all the time. When you get these thoughts that maybe he is doing drugs, ask a question "Is this my awareness? Is this my judgement?" If it is your judgement, POC and POD it. If it is an awareness, then you can ask "What choices do I have here?" Then you can look at what you really want to choose and if that choice works for you.

RECEIVING CONTRIBUTION

Caller: I'm wondering why money has been such a nuisance in my life. What else is possible?® How can I make money doing what I love? Why does money not come easily? What can I do to make money come easily? Why does it feel like I have been giving so much to people and whenever I receive, it is half the value of what I'm giving?

Nilofer: Truth: are you giving more than you are receiving? Everything that is will you destroy and uncreate it all? Right and Wrong, Good and Bad, POD, POC, All 9, Shorts, Boys and Beyonds®

What would it take for you to change this? What could I be or do different today to change this right away?

Truth: is money really a nuisance for you? Truth: where is money? Look at the money in your life and become aware of it. Look through your whole life and just go to a time where you created money with ease, where money just showed up with total ease. Get the energy of that.

What do you know about creating money with energy that you are pretending not to know or denying that you know, that if you were to know it would change everything for you? Everything that doesn't allow you to perceive, know, be and receive that, will you destroy and uncreate it all? Right and Wrong, Good and Bad, POD, POC, All 9, Shorts, Boys and Beyonds®

Get that energy of when you created money with total ease and expand that energy. Expand that energy to the size of the room you are in and down into Earth. Expand it to the size of the house you are in and down into Earth. Expand it to the size of the city you are in and down into Earth. Expand it to the size of the country you are in and down into Earth. Expand it to the size of Earth and beyond. Keep expanding that energy out.

What contribution can that energy be to your money flows? What contribution can your money flows be to it? As you ask for the contribution of that energy to your money flows, do you feel the expansion? Look at everything you have in your life. Look at your body. What contribution can your body be to your money flows and what contribution can you be to your body? Look at your home and everything that is in your home, all the things. What contribution can your home and everything in your home be to your money flows? What contribution can you be to your home and everything in your home? What contribution can your business be to your money flows and what contribution can you be to your business? What contribution can all the molecules of consciousness be to your money flows and what contribution can you be to all the molecules of consciousness?

As you ask everything for contribution and gift your contribution, you will begin to see everything shifting and changing. Do this little exercise every single day and then see what shows up for you.

KILLING YOUR CREATIONS

Caller: I am doing everything you recommended in the series and I do feel a lot of stuff changing. However, the money is not showing up. I do my money story every day, run all the questions as given. I appreciate everything that you have gifted to us.

Nilofer: The thought "However the money is not showing up" is a judgment. What if you were to get out of judgment? What if you were to be in the question "What else is possible here I haven't even considered?" You have a lot of stuff, which is showing up. As you go through the layers of it you are unlocking it, and there will be a tipping point at which everything will change.

When I first started creating money in my life, I used all the tools for 3 months. I used them every single day. Then after the 3 months, things started to change for me. Money started to show up. When you say "money is not showing up", you have actually just negated everything that you have done so far.

Everywhere you are judging whatever you are doing, will you destroy and uncreate it all? Right and Wrong, Good and Bad, POD, POC, All 9, Shorts, Boys and Beyonds®

Judgment will come up and when it does come up, POC and POD that. Ask, "What else is possible here?® What else can I be or do different here? What else is possible here that I haven't even considered?" These are my favorite questions.

I get that it is really easy to go into judgment, conclusions, separations, rejections, projections and all of that. I think being in the question is like a muscle. **You** have to build it. Keep playing with it. I do get that you just keep slipping, but just keep playing with it. The more you play with being in the question, the more you make choices, the more you are going to start changing things in your reality.

Ask that beautiful question "What would I like to create my life as?" Ask every single day, "What would I like to create my life as?" Pull energy into it and send out trickles of energy. When people find you, ask the energy to equalize. Do that exercise every single day and see what actually starts to shift and change and show up in your life.

Get the energy of everything in your life, you know – your bank accounts, your money flows, your credit cards, your whatever, everything related to money. Get the energy of all of that in front of you. Perceive that energy. Ask that energy "What can I contribute to you today? What can I receive from you today? What can I be or do different to change this right away?"

Hold your hands out wide and build the energy in your hands. More. More. More. Then say "1-2-3" and flick this lightening bolt of energy out at the count of 3. Repeat the "1-2-3" again. Repeat "1-2-3" again, and then repeat one more "1-2-3".

Become aware of the solidified futures that you've created around money. Then do a 1-2-3-4 on it. Go "1-2-3-4", "1-2-3-4", "1-2-3-4", "1-2-3-4". 1-2-3-4 is for changing the solidified futures.

Caller: When you say 'equalize the energy', what are you doing? Can you do that between people in a relationship?

Nilofer: When you are pulling energy or pulling massive amounts of energy from all over the universe, you send out trickles of energy to people all over the world who are looking for you and don't even know it. So these trickles of energy are sending out a very tiny part of the energy to all the people who are looking for you and don't even know it. When they find you, ask the energy to equalize. That means that the energy you are getting from the people and the energy they are getting from you becomes equal. Once that energy equalizes, there's a connection which is created. Both of you will contribute and receive equally from each other. They may become your repeat clients, your customers and so on.

You can do this in a relationship, as well. Pull energy from all over the universe through that person to you, then out behind you and send out trickles of energy to that person when the person is away from you. You will always be in their thoughts. When you are together, just equalize the energy flow. When you equalize the energy, you will have this sense of connection with that person which is quite amazing. How do you equalize the energy? Just ask for the energy flow to equalize.

I just love the energy flows because the energy flows are so amazing. It creates a sense of connection immediately for you.

If you start pulling energy from everything that is around you, you start to get a lot of information. The first part of that is that you push your barriers down. Then you start pulling energy from everything that is around you, and you start to get a lot of information. You will get information about maybe an appliance in your home that needs some attention. When you start to get the hits of energy of something wonky there, go to question, "What is this? What can I do with it? Can I change it? If so, how can I change it?"

Maybe you walk into a shop and you start pulling energy from the whole shop. You will get awarenesses of what kinds of deals are going on. You will get awarenesses of things you've been looking for. You'll find the most amazing thing which is there, and just go get it.

If I am travelling during the summer and looking at hotels, I pull energy from all the websites. I see everything that is listed and pull energy to see what is going to be a perfect fit for me. I pull in energy to find the best possible place and the best possible price. You can start pulling in energy when you are making bookings, etc. Then what tends to happens is that the human element – the person – makes a mistake. The universe will have your back. You'll find something gets over-ridden and you will literally end up with exactly what you are looking for.

When you are doing this and you experience a sense of confusion, it's because you don't have all the information.

Go to questions, "What information do I require here? Who do I call? Who can I talk to? Who can give me the information I am looking for?"

When you do that, you will start getting awarenesses of everything.

"What would you like to create your monetary reality as?" Be in question. "What would I like to create my money flows as? What would I like to create my money reality as? If I were choosing for me today, what would I create my money reality as?" These are a few questions you could play with.

One of the questions I've been asking every day is "What would I like to create my Access classes as?"
I realized how much I was buying into everybody else's points of views about how the classes should be, what I should be doing to promote the class, how many people there should be the class in order for me to feel successful about my classes and so on. Instead of asking "What is my reality with creating classes? What would I like to create my Access classes as? Or, what would I like to create my business as?"

When I first started doing the telesummit, I did everything how I thought it was supposed to be. It was so heavy for me. I was so stressed out all the time.

When I did the second telesummit, I thought "I don't care how people do it and whatever; I'm just going to do it because it's fun for me." I did it in a totally different way. I just created everything on the go. In 3 days, I had created my telesummit. In 5 days, I had my whole summit on. I did it at all times of the day and night, and it was just amazing! I had so much fun doing it. I made some money doing it too, which just floored me! That was creating my reality.

One of the things I am aware of is that my reality does not mean planning for something. I'll have a sense of what I would like to create. I might even have a sense of time-wise what I'd like to create. Yet the little elements in each, the things that you do every day to institute it, to create it, to actualize it and to maintain it; what works for me in my reality does not include planning for that too much in the future. I will wing it as I go. I'll just create something and as I'm doing it, I will keep adding and adding the required pieces to it. I create from chaos, and that really works for me.

That may not be your reality. Your reality may be that you like to have a little bit of order in your life. You like to create from that, and that works for you.

It is really important for you to get what *your* reality is with everything. Once you start to actually get what your reality is, you will start to actualize that reality. *Your* reality will be way greater than what you could have ever imagined. Play with this question, "What would I like to create my monetary reality as?" This is a question which I use every single day to create a lot of possibilities in my life. I suggest you use this. I can see the difference.

Caller: When would you push energy and is there a reason to do that in a money situation?

Nilofer: Pushing energy reminds me of the pushy sales person. When you go into a shop, you are ready to buy something, a salesperson comes up to you and is pushing at you to buy something, and you are like "I want to kill this guy! Why can't he go away?" I've literally had times when I've walked out of the shop, and not bought what I had actually gone in to buy in the first place because that person was being so pushy with me. So what the pushing energy basically does is push you out of the situation. It pushes you out of whatever it is that you are looking to create. Is that what you would really like to do?

There are a few situations in which I actually do use the pushing energy. One of them is when I see a traffic jam. There's a lot of traffic, so I push energy so the traffic will clear. Sometimes I will push energy if I don't want to have some person in my face. If I want someone to go away, I will temporarily push energy at them, because right at that situation I don't want to actually handle them. So I will push energy at them. Although, it's not so much as an 'energy push' as it is an 'energy flow'. You flow energy from behind you, through you to the person and out through the person. You can flow so much energy at the person that you fill them up. Their neediness disappears and the person will go away. So I will flow energy at people, I won't necessarily push.

Push is like creating a separation. When you flow energy at people, you are still maintaining a connection and honoring that person. It is as if you are saying "it doesn't work for me to have you with me right now." That's what an energy flow does. An energy push will actually create a separation between you and that person.

Have fun with this exercise. Practice the tools and stop judging it. Any time you are using these tools, you are creating a shift and change. Instead of going to judgement, go to question, "What can I choose here?" and "What else can I choose to change this?"

FACILITATING THE EARTH

For an exclusive interview with Special Guest Pam Houghteling, as she talks about our special capacities with Earth and how we can contribute and receive from Earth, visit http://www.moneycirclebook.com

CHAPTER SIX

BEING PRESENT

"Be Here NOW!" ~ Peggy Phoenix Dubro

"Consciousness includes everything without judgment. It is the willingness and capacity to be totally aware, totally present in all areas of your life." –Gary Douglas, founder of Access Consciousness ®

The first time that I read the above quote, I almost didn't register those words. As I'm looking at the past couple of weeks, I am aware of how *not* present I am.

Why is being present so important? When you are totally present in every moment of your life, you can totally receive. You can completely receive everything without judgment. You can receive all kinds of awareness. When you are totally present, then you will know exactly what is right now. You don't live in a fantasy world of what you think should be or what you think can be. What is present right now has the raw materials for giving you everything that you would like to create in your life, better than what you currently have and greater than what you can imagine. When you are completely present in the moment, you will realize that you have all the possible ingredients to create whatever it is that you desire to create in your life. In the present moment you are not doing a cop-out. You are not switching off your awareness and looking at the fantasy of what you think should be or what you hope should be.

Play:

Become aware of your feet on the floor. Now become aware of your back against the chair. Then become aware of your hands on your stomach. Any time you become aware that you are not present in your body; just become aware of three points in your body and you will be totally present.

The other tool for being present is really simple. Just tell yourself "Be here now."

When you are completely present, you will notice that no matter what is going on in the moment; you have all the ingredients to handle that, to actually move beyond that and to create a greater reality than anything you could have imagined. What else is possible here now that you haven't even considered? What else is possible here now that you haven't yet chosen? When you are totally aware, totally present with no judgment of you or anyone else, you have this intensity of awareness. When you are totally present, you actually have no judgment of you or anyone else.

I love going for a morning walk. I would go for my morning walk and have all these beautiful ideas. I could see all these beautiful possibilities. I noticed that I would just go into the future and not be present in my body. Every time I jumped out of my body, I would become aware of these three points of contact or say the words "be here now." I would immediately be present here in the now. All the ideas and possibilities that I was aware of, they were so much bigger than I perceived. I was aware of all the things that could contribute to making that idea actualize.

What else is possible with your money flows when you are more aware, more present and completely here now?

Whenever I am being present to everything in my life, it's almost like all those so called "problems" don't exist anymore. When I am completely here now, I always get an awareness of "all is well." I always have all the resources to be able to play with whatever is going on in my life. That has been the biggest gift that being present has given me.

The other thing opening up the more I am being present is I am actually more aware of the possibilities that exist for me. In the last 2 days alone, I have been creating and generating beyond anything that I have experienced before. I have all these possibilities that I am playing around with. As I look at the possibilities, I almost get a whole map of what I need to do and what energy I need to be to create everything I am looking at. That is so exciting. That is also because of being totally present.

Caller: I've had a long-standing, intimate relationship for years. When I split with this person – and it was an ugly breakup – unnecessary, and well, as far as I am concerned, my money went way down. Later on, I've had another mentor or advisor as a result of this relationship. My money flows ceased. The relationship also ended with a lot of lies and accusations on their part. I tried to explain what happened – my view of the situation – but they wouldn't listen. Now it is better, but not as I would like it to be. Whatever happened in any or both of these relationships is still bogging me down or affecting my money flows. What does it take to change this? If it is something that is beyond my awareness, how do I overcome it? Thank you for your contribution. I love you.

Nilofer: One of the things is that when people are angry with you, it affects your money flows. When people are happy with you, it contributes to your money flows. The first thing to do is just lower your barriers. As you lower them more and more, receive all the judgments that these people have about you. To "receive" means to lower your barriers and have no point of view about their judgment. When you think about these two people, are your barriers up or are your barriers down? Push your barriers down if you feel that they are up. When you have your barriers down, perceive the energy of the judgment that they have towards you. Have no point of view about that energy. What if you have no label to that energy?

What if you didn't call it anger, judgment or anything? What would that be? That energy would be just an energy. It's like free-form energy. You can use that energy to contribute to your money flows.

As you contribute that energy to your money flows, it expands. Now use that energy to contribute to any part of your life that you would like to. Use that energy to contribute to your business. Use that energy to create new clients and/or to create new possibilities in your business. Use that energy to contribute to the flow of sales in your business. Perceive the energy of your business and contribute that energy to the energy of your business. If you can perceive any area of your business where the energy is not moving, ask what can you be or do different to change that energy right away.

Now take that energy and actually contribute it to the two people that you were in relationship with? What can you give to them? What can you receive from them?

What if every so-called situation in your life is actually a huge gift that you are not acknowledging? Everything that doesn't allow you to perceive, know, be and receive the gift that every situation is in your life, will you destroy and uncreate it all? Right and Wrong, Good and Bad, POD, POC, All 9, Shorts, Boys and Beyonds®

EXPENSES INCREASED ALONG WITH INCOME

Caller: Over the last 6 weeks, my income has increased but so have the expenses. So it is still never enough. I still cannot pay all the bills even though the income has increased. What clearing or process can I use to destroy this pattern? Thank you.

Nilofer: Everything that is, will you destroy and uncreate it all? Right and Wrong, Good and Bad, POD, POC, All 9, Shorts, Boys and Beyonds®

The first thing to do is to sit down and actually know exactly what my expenses are every month and I'm very detailed about this. I suggest you do this. To your expenses you can add the 10% "I have money" account. It is an account where you take 10% of your income that you actually put away and don't spend, so you always *have* money. Also add a little money to it which is money for play. Make a really detailed account of your income, including your living expenses, the "I have money" account and some money to have fun with. Start asking for that amount of money to show up. When you start asking for that money to show up every month, then you cannot be in that place of "it is never enough". If you find that in the next month you have some expenses which have been added then you need to add that expense to the money you are asking for.

"What can I be or do different today to have X amount of money right away? And, What would it take for X amount of money to show up right away?" are two great questions that you can live by.

PLAYING WITH MONEY

Caller: I went to a casino to gamble just for fun, but I was aware that I was judging myself for gambling. I lost about $300. Also, I have some lotteries for a car - they are giving away a car every week – for me. I would like to go just for fun, but I go into the conclusion and expectation. So what can I ask or be different about not judging me, and also to go without expectations and still have fun? Thank you.

Nilofer: You have an awareness of what exactly is going on for you, and you are asking "how?" Once you have the awareness of it, you just make a choice. "I don't care what it takes; I'm not judging this anymore." Every time you have judgment come up, POC and POD, all the judgments around this, destroy and uncreate it all. Right and Wrong, Good and Bad, POD, POC, All 9, Shorts, Boys and Beyonds®

All the projections, expectations, separations, rejections and judgments that you have about going to the casino and about gambling, destroy and uncreate it all. Right and Wrong, Good and Bad, POD, POC, All 9, Shorts, Boys and Beyonds®

This is an ongoing work-in-progress. Every time you become aware of your projections and expectations, destroy and uncreate them. You can do it 30 times a day for the next 30 days.

The other question you can ask is "How much fun can I have gambling today?" All the judgments you have about gambling, will you destroy and uncreate them all? Right and Wrong, Good and Bad, POD, POC, All 9, Shorts, Boys and Beyonds®

Everywhere that you bought everyone else's points of view about gambling, will you destroy and uncreate it all? Right or Wrong, Good and Bad, POC and POD, All 9, Shorts, Boys and Beyonds.

What does gambling mean to you? Everything that is times godzillion destroy and uncreate it all. Right and Wrong, Good and Bad, POD, POC, All 9, Shorts, Boys and Beyonds®

There's a lot of charge in this, just keep using "What does gambling mean to me?" and keep POCing and PODing it for 30-100 times until it eases up for you. Once that charge is gone, ask "What projections, expectations, separations, rejections and judgments do I have about going to the casino and about gambling? Everything that brings up, destroy and uncreate it all. Right and Wrong, Good and Bad, POD, POC, All 9, Shorts, Boys and Beyonds®

How much fun can you have in the casino today and how much money can you make in the casino today? Everything that doesn't allow you to perceive, know, be and receive that, destroy and uncreate it all. Right and Wrong, Good and Bad, POD, POC, All 9, Shorts, Boys and Beyonds®

Before you go to the casino, ask yourself "Am I having fun right now?" If you are not having fun with that, then you why would choose that? Don't go there.

NO MONEY

Caller: I'd like to know if you can contribute to me with a clearing or a process. I feel stressed because I haven't made any money and the money that I receive I have to pay back right away for money I had to borrow last month for my rent. Now it's already half of the month and I don't have any clients. I've been asking questions, using some of the tools, and also asking "who does this belong to?" There's no change yet. Can you contribute on the same?"

Nilofer: Everything that is times godzillion will you destroy and uncreate it all? Right and Wrong, Good and Bad, POD, POC, All 9, Shorts, Boys and Beyonds®

All the oaths, vows, fealties, comealties, swearings, bindings, bondings and contracts that you have across all time, space, reality and dimensions about never having money, will you now revoke, recant, rescind, reclaim, renounce, denounce, destroy and uncreate it all? Right and Wrong, Good and Bad, POD, POC, All 9, Shorts, Boys and Beyonds®

Run this process 30 times a day for the next 30 days. Then go to question "What can I be or do different today to have money right away?" or "What would it take for money to show up with total ease, joy and glory right away?" Keep asking these questions. Every time you go to the conclusions, "Oh my God, money is not showing up" and when the money shows up, "I have to use it to pay" and any variations of those conclusions, destroy and uncreate it. POD and POC the conclusions.

What if every time you have this thought about having no money, you could destroy and uncreate it all? Everything that is times godzillion destroy and uncreate it all. Right and Wrong, Good and Bad, POD, POC, All 9, Shorts, Boys and Beyonds®

If all that you do is use this tool of destroying and un-creating every single thought, feeling and emotion you have about money today; everything will change for you. For the next 7 days, play with this tool.

Caller: Just last evening I came to a new awareness of how I had given all of my money away, more so than I ever have been willing to acknowledge. Every time money came to me or every time I generated or created money, I simply could not be with it. I could not let myself have it. I'm realizing I have no sense of being able to be with money just fully. I would like to change that now please. May I have some questions to facilitate shifting this?

Nilofer: How many lifetimes were you killed for having too much money? Everything that is times godzillion destroy and uncreate it all. Right and Wrong, Good and Bad, POD, POC, All 9, Shorts, Boys and Beyonds®

How many lifetimes were people who were close to you killed because of having too much money? Everything that is times godzillion will you destroy and uncreate it all? Right and Wrong, Good and Bad, POD, POC, All 9, Shorts, Boys and Beyonds®

All the oaths, vows, fealties, comealties, swearings, bindings, bondings and contracts you have to never have any money because of fear of death or destruction of you or your loved ones, will you now revoke, recant, rescind, reclaim, renounce, denounce, destroy and uncreate it all? Right and Wrong, Good and Bad, POD, POC, All 9, Shorts, Boys and Beyonds®

The other thing is "What does being with money mean to you? Everything that is times godzillion will you destroy and uncreate it all? Right and Wrong, Good and Bad, POD, POC, All 9, Shorts, Boys and Beyonds®

What does having money mean to you? Everything that is times godzillion will you destroy and uncreate it all? Right and Wrong, Good and Bad, POD, POC, All 9, Shorts, Boys and Beyonds®

What does having $1,000 mean to you? Everything that brings up or lets down, will you destroy and uncreate it all? Right and Wrong, Good and Bad, POD, POC, All 9, Shorts, Boys and Beyonds®

What does having $10,000 mean to you? Everything that is times godzillion will you destroy and uncreate it all? Right and Wrong, Good and Bad, POD, POC, All 9, Shorts, Boys and Beyonds®

What does having $50,000 mean to you? Everything that is times godzillion will you destroy and uncreate it all? Right and Wrong, Good and Bad, POD, POC, All 9, Shorts, Boys and Beyonds®

What does having $100,000 mean to you? Everything that is times godzillion will you destroy and uncreate it all? Right and Wrong, Good and Bad, POD, POC, All 9, Shorts, Boys and Beyonds®

What does having $250,000 mean to you? Everything that is times godzillion will you destroy and uncreate it all? Right and Wrong, Good and Bad, POD, POC, All 9, Shorts, Boys and Beyonds®

What does having half a million dollars mean to you? Everything that is times godzillion will you destroy and uncreate it all? Right and Wrong, Good and Bad, POD, POC, All 9, Shorts, Boys and Beyonds®

What does having one million dollars mean to you? Everything that is times godzillion will you destroy and uncreate it all? Right and Wrong, Good and Bad, POD, POC, All 9, Shorts, Boys and Beyonds.

What does having ten million dollars mean to you? Everything that is times godzillion will you destroy and uncreate it all? Right and Wrong,

Good and Bad, POD, POC, All 9, Shorts, Boys and Beyonds®

What does having fifty million dollars mean to you? Everything that is times godzillion will you destroy and uncreate it all? Right and Wrong, Good and Bad, POD, POC, All 9, Shorts, Boys and Beyonds®

What does having one hundred million dollars mean to you? Everything that is times godzillion will you destroy and uncreate it all? Right and Wrong, Good and Bad, POD, POC, All 9, Shorts, Boys and Beyonds®

Go back and repeat these clearings.

Notice what changed for you as you went through this exercise. If you keep doing this every day, it will actually increase your receiving for having that much money.

Caller: Hi, I just completed *Level 1*. I've been crying, feeling depressed, started not feeling good enough. I've settled for less all my life. I'm aware I have been waiting for some day. I've worked hard all my life and never made enough money. I have such strong issues around money; it makes me cry and sick to my stomach. I destroy and uncreate it. I don't know where to turn to anymore. I am terrified and hopeless.

Nilofer: Everything that you are perceiving, who does it belong to? When you go to an Access Consciousness® class, just be aware that you come out of the class even more aware than before. In this world what do you have more? Do you have more joy, happiness and fun? Or do you have more sadness, depression, drama and trauma? So what are you going to be aware of? You are going to be aware of other people's stuff.

Everything that is, return it all back to sender with consciousness attached. Right and Wrong, Good and Bad, POD, POC, All 9, Shorts, Boys and Beyonds®

What energy, space and consciousness can your body and you be to be the energy, space and consciousness you truly be for all eternity? Everything that doesn't allow you to perceive, know, be and receive that, destroy and uncreate it all. Right and Wrong, Good and Bad, POD, POC, All 9, Shorts, Boys and Beyonds®

Run it 30 times a day for the next 30 days. This will start to give you a sense of peace and ease with all those feelings and emotions you're perceiving.

Look at your story about money. Everything that is, will you destroy and uncreate it all? Right and Wrong, Good and Bad, POD, POC, All 9, Shorts, Boys and Beyonds®

In your *Foundation* and *Level 1* manual, look at all the materials you have about creating money, everything to do with money, all the clearings, everything. Read it and re-read it. Apply everything that is there on those pages. Take those clearings, put them on an audio loop, and keep listening to them over and over again.

Run your money bar every single night for the next 6-7 months. A lot of things will start to change for you.

Every time you have a thought, feeling or emotion about money, destroy and uncreate it all. Right and Wrong, Good and Bad, POD, POC, All 9, Shorts, Boys and Beyonds®

I had this cough. It was a persistent cough which was going on for almost 2-3 weeks. I would suddenly start coughing for no reason. Since this had been going on for so long, I said to myself, "I don't care what it takes, this has to change." When I went into that energy of being a demand for it to change, I had this awareness of "what if I were to become aware of exactly what thoughts, feelings and emotions were going on through my mind as I start to cough?" I started doing that. I became more present and more aware of what was going on in my mind every time I coughed. Every time I coughed, I would go "What am I thinking right now? What am I feeling right now? Oh it's that. Everything that is, destroy and uncreate it all. Right and Wrong, Good and Bad, POD, POC, All 9, Shorts, Boys and Beyonds®"

I did it every single time I coughed. In a few days, my cough was gone. What if you were to be that vigilant with all your thoughts, feelings and emotions about money? Every time you had that emotion coming up, or thought or feeling, or whatever, what if you were to go, "everything that is, destroy and uncreate it all. Right and Wrong, Good and Bad, POD, POC, All 9, Shorts, Boys and Beyonds®"

POINTS OF VIEW CREATE YOUR REALITY

Caller: Hi, I so would have loved to go to Florida to be with Dr. Dain Heer's *Being You* class. Of course, it didn't happen. It's in a few days and my heart is deeply sad. The money didn't show up. I asked the universe. It seems the universe does not hear me. What if I don't make it even using the tools of Access? What can I do to stay strong and not give up?

Nilofer: "It seems the universe doesn't hear me." You have a point of view about what is going to happen! Everything that is, will you destroy and uncreate it all? Right and Wrong, Good and Bad, POD, POC, All 9, Shorts, Boys and Beyonds®

This is the biggest thing which will stop your money flow, or more succinctly this is the biggest thing which will stop your receiving. We ask for things to show up, and then we judge when they don't show up. We have kind of defined a time frame in which those things have to show up. Every time you judge it, you are killing the energy. You are killing your receiving.

When you ask for something to show up, the universe replies, "Oh wow! You are asking for that. Come on. Let me rearrange myself to make sure that you get that." Yet, the next minute if the Universe hears, "Oh, I'm never getting it." the universe responds, "They are asking for 'I'm never getting it', let me rearrange myself to give you exactly what you are asking for." If you are sending out these conflictual signals to the universe, that's exactly what the universe is going to give you.

A couple of years back, I wanted to do my facilitator's training. There was this whole list of prerequisites for doing the training. I looked at it, and then wrote down every telecall series I had to do or all the required pre-requisites. I wrote down all the expenses that each one of those entailed. I wanted to go for facilitator's training in Australia, which was like about 3-4 months away.

Every time I thought about that, it just felt really heavy to me. I still wanted to go. What I had was an awareness that I could not. It was an awareness that it was not the time for me to go. That's the reason it was heavy. The other reason was that the amount of money at that point of time for me was really huge. I could not go to a point of believing that I could create that money in those 3 months.

Basically, I let go of my projections, expectations, separations, rejections and judgments about going to Australia in 3 months to do that training. I was just in the question "What would it take for me to go to a facilitators training?" In January, the money literally showed up. I could just choose and go for whichever facilitators' training after that I wanted to go to.

What if you were to not have a time frame for anything? What if you were to actually ask for something and have no expectations about it? When you start doing that, when you start to ask for things and have no expectations around it, what often starts to happen is that those things that you are asking for will show up.

I once heard Gary (Douglas, the founder of Access Consciousness®) say in class that "everything that I have been asking for has started to show up in the last 5 years." When I heard that I went, "wow, I'd like that." Six months after that, I realized that everything I was asking for was actually showing up.

What if you were to ask and actually receive everything that you have ever asked for? That will happen when you have no judgments about when it shows up or how it shows up. What I have seen is that every time I ask for something, it shows up way greater than I could have ever imagined.

Write down 10 things that you would like to create with money. It could be like a course you want to take. It could be travel. It could be buying something for you. It could be paying off your bills or your past expenditure. Whatever it is, just write down 10 things that you would like to have money for, or 10 things that you would like to create or do with money. Then, for each one of those things, make it into a question "What would it take for me to have this right away? What can I be or do different today to have this right away?"

In your case, it could be, "What would it take for me to attend a *Being You* class right away? Or ask, "What can I be or do different today to attend a *Being You* class right away?" Everything that doesn't allow that I destroy and uncreate it all. Right and Wrong, Good and Bad, POD, POC, All 9, Shorts, Boys and Beyonds®

Read those 10 questions that you have written down every single day. The other thing is to be grateful for everything that shows up in your life, no matter what it is.

In those 3-4 months, while I was asking to go for facilitators' training, I actually had my list of questions of everything I would like to create. Every single day I wrote a gratitude list of 10 new things that I am grateful for today. Very soon I noticed I was so grateful all the time; and because I was so grateful, I was so aware of just how much I was receiving. That changed everything for me.

STOP HEAD TRIPPING

Caller: So, I'm aware of being present in my body instead of being in my head, which allows me to be more efficient and playful. What would it take for me to take advantage of the greater possibilities and stop head-tripping? Thanks.

Nilofer: Every time you have an awareness that you are in your head and not being present, just become aware of 3 points of contact with your body. You will become present. It's a muscle that you have to build. It may be one of the most difficult things that you will do. Although, I wonder what it would take for that to be easy for you. Anyway, just choose this every time you become aware of head-tripping: become present in your body.

STOP JUDGING YOURSELF

Caller: How do I not judge myself?

Nilofer: You can do that by making a demand that no matter what it takes, I am never, ever, ever going to judge myself. It is just a choice. Each time that judgment shows up, be aware. Remind yourself, "Oh, I'm judging myself. Never mind, I am not choosing that anymore." Sometimes, that's what you have to do. That's what you will do when you are that demand, "no matter what it takes."

Then be willing to do whatever it takes to stop judging. That's when you'll actually stop judging yourself. It's a work-in-progress.

Every time you judge yourself, destroy and uncreate that, and choose not to judge yourself. This is, again, one of the most difficult things that you will do (although, what if it could be ease, joy and glory?). Yet, it is that thing which will give you the greatest amount of freedom in your life.

Caller: Earlier you said if I ask the questions, any one of them you mentioned, I don't have to know the answer. Just keep asking and see what shows up. I have ideas, but without a good paying job, I don't see how I can ever make them a reality. I really want my life to change because I really don't know why I am on this Earth. Actually I love Earth. It's my life I hate.

Nilofer: How many points of view do you have about how you can receive money? You came to a conclusion saying that "because I don't have a good-paying job, I can't have money." Have you really held the doors open to receiving with this question? Everything that is, will you destroy and uncreate it all? Right and Wrong, Good and Bad, POD, POC, All 9, Shorts, Boys and Beyonds®

The other thing that you are saying is that "I hate my life on the Earth". When you say that, that's exactly what you are creating. What if you went into gratitude for your life? "What am I grateful for in my life today?" Look at the small things. "Oh, you know, I'm grateful that I live in this beautiful part of the world and I'm grateful for the cold winter. I'm grateful for the hot summer. I'm grateful that I'm sitting here listening to this Money Circle call. I'm grateful for the people I have in my life." Start doing the grateful list, 10 new things in your life that you are grateful for, every day. Soon you will become aware of just how much you actually have in your life. When you start getting to that place, and you are in that space of gratitude, you will start to have more and more and more showing up. Why? You are willing to be grateful for and to acknowledge everything that is showing up in your life.

ARE YOU GETTING HOOKED?

Caller: Hi, Nilofer. Somebody did call me and ask to be facilitated. Then she got really upset with me. She said "how did you get so good?" I didn't even think I was good. I was only in Access for a few months. It made me uncomfortable. It seems like I somehow got hooked. Is there a clearing to let that go? Thank you for being here.

Nilofer: We kind of get hooked for all kinds of things. I've been so amazed this last week because I am seeing the insane places that we choose to get hooked on. Everything that is, will you destroy and uncreate it all? Right and Wrong, Good and Bad, POD, POC, All 9, Shorts, Boys and Beyonds®

Truth: were you aware of her judgment of herself of not being good enough? Everywhere you bought into all those judgments and locked them in place in your life, your living, your future, your reality and your body; everything that is, will you destroy and uncreate it all now and re-turn it all back to sender with consciousness attached? Right and Wrong, Good and Bad, POD, POC, All 9, Shorts, Boys and Beyonds®

Next time you are having a conversation with anybody, what if you just pushed your barriers down and received all their judgments? I wonder what that would create in your universe. Let go of whatever it is that you are holding on to.

Caller: After lowering my barriers last week, I noticed that receiving food is very easy for me. What will it take to receive money as easily as food? I received food from so many unexpected places. It was very interesting. I've noticed it a little in the past whenever I have gone on my diet. I will stop eating sugar, and people would offer me all kinds of candy. This time, I received different kinds of food. How can I change the food to money?

Nilofer: The first thing is you have to acknowledge that you lowered your barriers and were willing to receive more. So, more food showed up in your life. Every time you are receiving something go "Wow! Thank you, universe for giving me this and what would it take for more than this to show up? What would it take for 10 times this to show up?"

Then you could go to this place of "How can I change the food to money?" You are saying that, "I can receive this, but I would like to receive something else." What if you were willing to receive everything and have no judgment? Do you notice how even when we are receiving, we start to throw up our barriers to stop ourselves from receiving. Just go to this place of "Everything that is, destroy and uncreate it all. Right and Wrong, Good and Bad, POD, POC, All 9, Shorts, Boys and Beyonds®"

Just lower your barriers, receive everything and ask for more to show up. Say, "Thank you, universe, for giving me all this food. What would it take to have money and more food show up in my life?"

Caller: When I get judged by others, it's very uncomfortable being in the same space as them. It's like I'm on guard, keeping barriers down is not easy. They keep going up.

Nilofer: It's a practice. When you feel uncomfortable around others and you keep pushing your barriers down; you still perceive this energy of uncomfortableness. Are you actually perceiving the judgment that they have about them?

I noticed myself that when I stepped into the elevator or lift, sometimes I felt just at ease standing with whoever was there with me in the elevator. Sometimes I was getting really, really uncomfortable. So I asked myself, "Truth: are my barriers up or down?" I got the awareness that my barriers were down. I went "Wow! My barriers are down and I'm still feeling uncomfortable!" Then I went to the next question, "Is this mine?" Immediately it just lightened up. That uncomfortable energy was actually not me. Much of what I perceived was actually the other person or the other people who were there in the elevator with me. And when I actually acknowledged that, that energy started to change for me. So, when you perceive that people are judging you, is it them judging you, or is it them judging themselves and you just being aware of that?

Practice lowering your barriers. Push your barriers down. Then you will have an awareness of their judgment of judging themselves. Ninety-nine percent of the time when people are judging you, they are actually judging themselves. So when I get the awareness, I think "Wow, this is them judging them. How does it get any better than that? It is not even relevant to me." And I just get off it.

Caller: I have been judged since I was a child, and I judged myself harshly. Now my barriers won't stay down. What do I do?

Nilofer: You have to go "I don't care what it takes! Judgment is not going to be a part of my universe." Then you do barriers down every time that you have point of view or you have judgment about yourself. To dissipate the energy, think "Interesting point of view, I have this point of view. Interesting point of view, I have this point of view." Keep repeating, "Interesting point of view, I have this point of view" until that point of view or judgment disappears. Every time you perceive somebody as judging you, you can use this *Interesting point of view* (iPOV) tool. Keep saying that until that judgment disappears.

Use the following for the next 6 months.

There are three tools here:
1. Demand to change it,
2. Lower your barriers, and
3. Interesting Point of View.

RUNNING YOUR MONEY BAR WHILE YOU SLEEP

Caller: I know how to run The Bars®, but how do you just run that one Bar?

Nilofer: You can ask for any three bars to turn on every night when you go to sleep. Don't ask for more than 3 bars to turn on. You just ask for any three bars to turn on. Think to yourself, "Power band turn on." Then select any other 2 bars. You could think "Money bar, connect to the power band." The one I use to run was gratitude. "Gratitude bar, connect to the power band." "Creativity bar, connect to the power band." Then ask them to run all night long.

In other words, every night before you go to sleep you ask the 3 bars to run through the night. When I was playing with this, I would run 3 bars in the night and 3 bars in the daytime. I would have 3 bars running all the time. I did this for about 8 or 9 months. It created a huge shift in my universe. Basically, you don't have to touch anything; you just ask the 3 bars to turn on and run.

Running your Money Bar every night while you sleep will erase the points of view, beliefs and considerations around money. You will have a different awareness.

STEPS TO JOYFULLY CREATE A PHENOMENAL LIFE & LIVING

Join Glenyce Hughes as she uses the tools of Access Consciousness® and transformative exercises to guide you to choose, create and activate your body, life, money flows, business, relationships and so much more!

Visit http://www.moneycirclebook.com

CHAPTER SEVEN

THE ENERGY OF THE FUTURE POSSIBILITIES

"The futures you desire to create become possible when you make enough money to change realities. How much money would that be for you? Where can you start today?" ~ Gary Douglas

One of the things I heard Gary Douglas, the founder of Access Consciousness®, state is "the future that is possible is way greater than the future you can imagine." Every time I heard it, this just felt like -- it almost felt like my hair is standing on my body. This was like it gave me the chills and the goose bumps. I have been in question about this for a really long time. I am kind of starting to get what he was saying when he said that. The future that is possible is way greater than the future we can ever imagine. Are you willing to tap into that future? Are you willing to get the energy of the Future Possibilities?

So, let's do a little exercise. Just close your eyes and get the energy of the Future Possibilities. Perceive, know, be and receive that energy. How is that energy? What can you perceive the energy as? Is it expansive, infinite and really awesome? What if, for the next 7 days at different points in the day, you were to tap into the energy of the Future Possibilities? When you perceive that energy, will you ever go back to your stories, the trauma and drama of your reality anymore?

What physical actualization of the phenomenance of the Future Possibilities are you now capable of generating, creating and instituting? Everything that doesn't allow you to perceive, know, be and receive that, will you destroy and uncreate it all? Right and Wrong, Good and Bad, POD, POC, All 9, Shorts, Boys and Beyonds®

For the next 7 days, your home-play is to tap into the energy of the Future Possibilities. Get the energy of the Future Possibilities at different times during the day. Also, run the above process that I just shared with you.

WHAT IS YOUR REALITY?

Creating your own reality is actually having your own reality, which is different from what this reality is all about. Ever since we are born, there are these things which are projected at us. People have expectations of us, and we grow up buying into this reality. We grow up thinking that this is our reality and everything that we even ask for is actually not our own reality. When you start asking for your own reality to show up, what shows up is totally different than what you have been living all these years. You start creating your own reality by going to question. The question that I love, that I have been working with over the past few months, is "If I were being me today, what would I create? What would I choose?"

Once you start being in that question, pieces and parts of your own reality start to show up. One of the things that I have noticed about having my own reality show up is all these things show up. Things that have me think, "Oh, I didn't even know I was looking for this! Yet, this is just so perfect! This is exactly what I require and what I desire!"

When I first started doing Access about two and a half years ago, I remember, after doing my first set of core classes (which are *Bars*, *Foundation* and *Level 1*), I was asking for a new house show up. About a month or so after the classes, one of my friends called me up and said "Hey! We haven't met in a while. Do you want to meet?" She said she was going to look at some houses and asked if I'd like to come along. I went with her to see the houses.

Both of us didn't like any of the houses we saw. As we were talking to the realtor, I jokingly asked "Do you have a 3-bedroom apartment here?" She said she did and took us to see that 3-bedroom apartment. The moment I walked into the house, my whole energy just expanded out. When I looked at what was there in the house, I looked at the different things and it was just perfect! This house had all those things that I didn't even know that I was looking for. That's what happens when your own reality starts to show up for you.

Look at your whole life. Look at what's going on in your life. Look back and catch those magical moments where you had your own reality. Get at least one instance of when your reality actually showed up.

Caller: My own reality, now that I've really seen the Access tools, is that I just know that I have to be aware of what I ask for. Even when things are not going good, I just acknowledge that I'm creating it. If I'm creating something that I don't like, I recognize it and I acknowledge it. Then I just see if I'm willing to create something bigger, something different and more expansive for me and for my life, which is going to be a huge contribution in a different way. I'm not in the polarity, like this is right and this is wrong. I'm just being aware, "what else can I choose now in a different way?" I'm aware of whatever it is that I'm creating. So I don't feel like a victim. But I'm aware that everything that I'm creating is all about me.

Nilofer: Notice that you are going to this space of "I'm willing to see the good, the bad and the ugly of me and my life with no judgment?" with this place of "Everything is just an interesting point of view."

You must've had little moments of when something magical has actually showed up in your life. When it did, you went, "Wow! I didn't even know I was looking for this, but this is just perfect for what's showing up in my life right now!"

CREATOR

Caller: About a year and a half ago, I wanted to move from a one-bedroom apartment. I just asked that I wanted to move to a 3-bedroom home to rent. I was just asking "where is this home going to be? Who wants to rent a home for these 3 Austin people – my son, my boyfriend and me?" And then a month and a half later, we found a house for rent. I didn't even have the money to move. I didn't even have the money for the deposit. But the money showed up. Even the landlord said "You know, just move and I will charge you half of the money for rent for December." It was the middle of November and he said, "You can move. You don't have to pay any rent in December, you only pay me half and you can start paying your rent in January." So, that was like my Thanksgiving gift. It just showed up. Yeah, so how does it get any better than that?

Nilofer: We've created these moments in our life. Can you see that this is part of your own reality showing up? This is not about you buying into what this reality is where everything is trauma, drama, pain, suffering and gory. When you create your own reality, you create things almost like magic.

Everywhere you have not acknowledged 'you' as this awesome creator of magic, and all the magic that you have, and this capacity to create your own reality; will you destroy and uncreate it all? Will you perceive, know, be and receive all those moments when you were actually creating your own reality? Right and Wrong, Good and Bad, POD, POC, All 9, Shorts, Boys and Beyonds®

Can you perceive that energy of your own reality? Just get that energy of your own reality and magnify it. Just step it up more and more. Keep on expanding it until you feel your heart open up. Get that energy in front of you. Now start pulling more and more energy from all over the universe into this energy. Send out trickles of this energy to everyone in this universe who is looking for you and doesn't even know that they are looking for you. When they find you, ask this energy to equalize.

This is about you actually beginning to create your own reality. What if you were to do this exercise every single day?

One of my clients shared this beautiful question, which she has been in for the past few months. I just loved it.

"What is beyond this reality that I haven't yet chosen?"

When you talk about "beyond this reality" that is actually you having your own reality. What if you could be in this question for the next 7 days and see what started to open up for you?

"What is beyond this reality that I haven't yet chosen? Everything that doesn't allow me to perceive, know, be and receive that, I destroy and un-create it all. Right and Wrong, Good and Bad, POD, POC, All 9, Shorts, Boys and Beyonds®'"

I DON'T HAVE ENOUGH

Caller: I have two questions. I have been using a lot of the tools that you gave us. Even though the things have been changing, and I'm grateful for the change, I'm still having that energy of "I'm not having enough." And I have to be stressing at the end of every month to hurry to come out with the money to pay the bills and rent. What else is possible here that I'm not getting?

Nilofer: What if you were to not go to the judgment? What if you were to stay in the gratitude and to acknowledge all the changes that are showing up? Try writing down 5 new things that you are grateful for today. When you start acknowledging 5 new things that you are grateful for every day, what will start to happen is that you will begin to come to this energy of how much you actually have in your life. When I started doing this, I very quickly moved from this place of "I don't have, I don't have, I don't have…" to "Oh my God, I have this, and I have this, and I have this, and I have this!" My whole energy changed to "Oh my God, I have so much in my life."

What if you could acknowledge the little things that are showing up in your life and be grateful for them? For instance "Oh my God, I'm so grateful for when it's so hot out there I'm sitting in my house, in my home, which is air-conditioned, and I'm sitting in this place, which is feeling so comfortable for me. How did I get to be so lucky to have this?"

Acknowledge all the small things, which I'm sure you have in your life. Soon you will move to the energy of how much you actually have, which kind of breaks this whole cycle of "I don't have. I don't have. I don't have."

When you are being here now, when you feel yourself going into that place of stress and worry about your money to pay the bills; what if you were to just be aware of the 3 points of contact with your body? Your feet on the floor, your back against the chair and your hands against your thigh, and be here now. When you are totally present, totally aware in this moment, there is no space for worry or fear to show up.

So these are the two things for you: 1) five things you are grateful for today and 2) every time you have the worry, just come back to total awareness and being present in the moment.

MONEY AND KIDS

Caller: The second question: I have a 15 year old son. He's very good at receiving money. Yet, when it comes to buying something for him or his body for fun, he doesn't want to do it. He'll choose to expand his money in video games. He just loves that and doesn't care how much money he gives away for that. And yes, the place is set. I know myself that what can

I ask there or clear that I'm judging him and also judging me. This I feel is my block.

Nilofer: All the projections, expectations, separations, rejections and judgments that you have about your son, about how he should be living his life, and how he should be spending his money; will you destroy and uncreate it all? Right and Wrong, Good and Bad, POD, POC, All 9, Shorts, Boys and Beyonds®

Everything that his relationship was with you yesterday, will you destroy and uncreate it all? Right and Wrong, Good and Bad, POD, POC, All 9, Shorts, Boys and Beyonds®

He is an infinite being. As an infinite being, can he make his own choices? What if there is no such thing as a wrong choice? What if every choice was creating awareness? He is making choices, which are contributing to him. And maybe he is making choices which are not contributing to him. Yet the more you empower him to make his own choices, you are actually giving him a bigger gift. The biggest gift is that he has choice.

When you look back over your life at what people have expected of you and projected at you, either your parents, your partner or whoever, they wanted you to do something that you absolutely didn't want to do. You wanted to do something, and they were like "don't do it." How much of a constriction did that create in your universe? If you had that place of "I can choose whatever it is that I'd like to choose," how different would your life be? Can you do that for your son?

One of the things that I love to use with myself is this clearing: "What energy, space and consciousness can my body and I be to stop protecting my kids for all eternity? Everything that doesn't allow me to perceive, know, be and receive that, destroy and uncreate it all. Right and Wrong, Good and Bad, POD, POC, All 9, Shorts, Boys and Beyonds®"

Every time I find myself going to that place, I just run this clearing on me. Everything just shifts and changes for me. We give our kids pocket money and let them choose what they wish to buy.

I remember that my son, who is 11 years old, wanted to buy some games for his PS3. We went into this shop. He's looking at the games and found a game which is to do with fighting. My husband was standing next to him, and obviously did not want my son to buy the game. My son started to get adamant over it. So I just started having this conversation with him. The questions I gave him were "If I buy this, what will my life be like in 5 years' time? And if I don't buy this, what will my life be like in 5 years' time?"

My son asked himself the two questions. He said, "No, I don't want that." Then he looked at a few other games that he was interested in. Every game he looked at, he realized, "No, if I buy this my life is going to contract." Until he came to this game that was a football game. The moment he asked the questions about that game, his energy kind of just expanded out.

Then he told me "You know, mom, I have this game. I have the demo version of this game. I've been playing this game, and I just love it!" It's like his whole world just expanded out and he actually bought that game.

Now I realize that if that day my husband had said "no, you can't buy that game because it's all fighting and stuff like that", my son would have actually fought for and defended his choice that he was making. He would have ended up just buying it. But I was absolutely okay with him to buy that game. I was willing to go to that place of actually asking him the two questions, which shifted and changed everything for him.

What if you could ask your son a question and see what shifts and changes for him? What if you could actually honor whatever choice he's making, no matter what choice he's making? We look at our kids, look at some of the choices they are making, and think "wow, you know, I don't think that choice is going to work." Yet, what if you were willing to just step back and honor them for whatever choice they are making? Maybe the choice they are making is working for them. Maybe it's not, but choice creates awareness.

If you actually step back, they will stop fighting you, which will actually create awareness in their life. The next choice they make will be completely different. See how that works for you. And I totally, totally get that whole thing about getting freaked out about what choices your kids are making, but that's one of the joys of being a mother.

You can, also, have this same sort of allowance with your significant other, your partner, your mother or all those people in your life.

What energy, space and consciousness can your body and you be to stop protecting your loved ones for all eternity? Everything that is times godzillion will you destroy and uncreate it all? Right and Wrong, Good and Bad, POD, POC, All 9, Shorts, Boys and Beyonds®

WHO OR WHAT ARE YOU UNWILLING TO BE?

Caller: I'm having difficulty asking for money for my services. It comes to me and I just give it away, even though I do want to charge for my services. I'm doing things on a sliding scale. So I try to make it really reasonable. Yet it's been eluding me to actually receive money for my services.

Nilofer: Say 10 time, "I'd like to have the money now please." Just ask, "Can I have the money now please?" Do you actually desire to have a sliding scale or would you just like to have money?

Run these couple of clearings which help clear energy about being a "rich whore" and "rich bitch."

What stupidity are you using to create the lack of being the rich whore you are choosing? Everything that is times godzillion will you destroy and uncreate it all? Right and Wrong, Good and Bad, POD, POC, All 9, Shorts, Boys and Beyonds®

What stupidity are you using to create the lack of being the rich bitch you are choosing? Everything that is times godzillion will you destroy and uncreate it all? Right and Wrong, Good and Bad, POD, POC, All 9, Shorts, Boys and Beyonds®

That energy you are unwilling to be will create lack of money in your life. When you have any of your judgments around this show up, start running this clearing for yourself.

What is a whore? A whore is a person who is willing to receive money for services rendered. So if you are not willing to be a "rich whore" or a "rich bitch," you will actually not be able to receive money.

Actually, the things you won't do or you won't be, create what you want to see. If you are judging that you can't be a whore, it's a place where you create not being able to receive anything that a whore would receive, which includes money for services rendered.

So, what stupidity are you using to create the lack of being the controlling rich bitch you are choosing? Everything that is times godzillion will you destroy and uncreate it all? Right and Wrong, Good and Bad, POD, POC, All 9, Shorts, Boys and Beyonds®

What stupidity are you using to create the lack of being the rich whore you are choosing? Everything that is times godzillion will you destroy and uncreate it all? Right and Wrong, Good and Bad, POD, POC, All 9, Shorts, Boys and Beyonds®

Caller: But I think, "People can't afford this. It's a luxury item."

Nilofer: Do you have a point of view that you have to offer affordable services? Would you like to give up that people can't afford this and it's a luxury item? This is so funny. We go to this place of what people can or can't afford. I have done things like that. Then I will see someone go to somebody else and pay a much bigger amount to buy a product or service that somebody else is selling. Is it truth that people can't afford it or is it that you are projecting your points of view on them?

All your projections, expectations, separations, rejections and judgments about what people can afford or cannot afford to pay for your services; will you destroy and uncreate it all? Right and Wrong, Good and Bad, POD, POC, All 9, Shorts, Boys and Beyonds®

What is the figure that you would like to charge for your services? Say you thought $70. Then ask "Truth: what would the service like to be charged?" It could be $30 or is it $130? Say you came up with $130.

Everywhere you are going into your head to find the answer instead of just knowing what the service would like to be charged, will you destroy and uncreate it all? Right and Wrong, Good and Bad, POD, POC, All 9, Shorts, Boys and Beyonds®

CRAZY PHRASE

Do the crazy phrase.

"Everything is the opposite of what appears to be, nothing is the opposite of what appears to be." Say this 10 times.

After this crazy phrase, once again ask "Truth: what would your service like to be charged?" Maybe you'll come up with a bigger price, say $135. That's what your service would like to be charged.

Now the question is can you receive $135 for your service?

"What does charging $135 for my service mean to me? Everything that is times godzillion destroy and uncreate it all. Right and Wrong, Good and Bad, POD, POC, All 9, Shorts, Boys and Beyonds®

Do this 30 times a day for the next 30 days. See what shifts for you. You'll find that as you start doing this, you will have all those points of view showing up which are why you can't be charging that much for your service. As the points of view show up, you destroy and uncreate them all. As those points of view shift and change, you will actually be able to receive that money for your services.

The other thing that might happen as you POC and POD those points of view, you'll again ask the service "What would you like to be charged?" The amount it would like to be charged may go up. When that amount goes up, you change your figure to that.

I used to teach yoga. I had this thing of "Oh my God, I have to make this really affordable for people." So I had priced it at just $20 a month. People could come for 8 classes with me at $20 a month. To make it even more attractive to people, I said, "well, if you miss any classes, you can make up those classes." So I had people who had paid me $20 that came for the next six months because they had not done those 8 classes. I would go for these classes and people would not show up or there would be just one or two people. That was just such a dishonoring of me and my time. Then I learned a healing modality. I decided to take on one client. It just felt so heavy to me to be charging that little amount of money, so I began to charge about $50 for one session. That was a huge jump from $20 for 8 sessions to $50 per session.

At that time I didn't have Access tools. I knew EFT, which is a modality where you tap on all these points on your face and head while saying some statements. I started practicing EFT while saying, "I now charge

150 dirham ($40 or $50) per session." I would tap on all the points every day, 10-15-20 times.

By the time I had done it for a week, I offered one of my friends, "Hey, why don't you come try out the session?" Until that time I was giving away free sessions to all my friends. She not only agreed to come, but also to pay for it. She came for a session and didn't even ask me how much I was charging for the session. At the end of the session, I was like so fearful and so nervous whether she was going to pay me or not. Then she said, "So how much should I pay you?" I said "$50." She opened her purse, gave me the money, and then asked "When can I come for the next session?" I almost like dropped out of my chair. For me, that was like "Yes, now I can receive this money."

Just play with this. "What does charging XYZ mean to me?" Do it 30 times a day for the next 30 days. Notice what starts to show up in your life.

MORE CLEARINGS

What would it take for me to make thousands of dollars from everything I do every day? Everything that doesn't allow me to perceive, know, be and receive that, will I destroy and uncreate it all? Right and Wrong, Good and Bad, POD, POC, All 9, Shorts, Boys and Beyonds®

What would it take for me to have something that is nurturing for me as a being and would make me more money than I never imagined possible? Everything that doesn't allow me to perceive, know, be and receive that, will I destroy and uncreate it all? Right and Wrong, Good and Bad, POD, POC, All 9, Shorts, Boys and Beyonds®

You have to get to this place of "I don't care what it takes; I'm going to just stop myself from limiting money." Then money just shows up. It's like that with money, with relationships, with everything. When you go to this place of demand, "I don't care! This thing in my life has to change," that's when you are willing to have it.

What would happen if you had too much money? What choice could you make that would allow more money in your life? Choice, question, possibility and contribution: you have to function from these four. Choose: "I'm going to have this money. I don't know how I'm going to do it. I don't know, but whatever it takes, I'm going to get this. I'm willing to have this from every source under the sun."

When I look back at all the things that I have created in my life, a lot of times it was all these places where I went, "This thing has to change. I have to have this, and I don't care what has to happen for this to occur." Many times it is actually what you are being or doing that allows you to change it. You are not actually asking the universe to change, although you are asking the universe to give you what you would like. You are saying, "I don't care what it takes. I don't care who or what I have to be or do different. This thing has to change in my life, and I am going to have this."

Two years back, I looked at what was happening with my money situation. I had a little money coming in and then it would stop. Then it would come and then it would stop. Then I would have to spend the whole money before I went to actually create something new. I said to me, "You know what? This has to change. I don't care what has to happen, but this has to change." Then I created having those things show up in my life, which actually, you know, facilitated me in changing that. Then I ended up doing a couple of telecalls. My whole monetary reality changed with that. So you have to be willing to just go to that place and demand "I don't care what has to happen, but this thing has to change."

The other thing is, "Would you be willing to be the richest person in your family that everybody came to get money from?" Everything that brings up or lets down, will you destroy and uncreate it all? Right and Wrong,

Good and Bad, POD, POC, All 9, Shorts, Boys and Beyonds®

When you are unwilling to be the richest person in your family, and when you are unwilling to be in a place of having other people come to ask you for money, you are actually stopping your money flows. Connect to a time when somebody came and asked you for money that you didn't want to give them. Everything that brings up or lets down, will you destroy and uncreate it all? Right and Wrong, Good and Bad, POD, POC, All 9, Shorts, Boys and Beyonds®

Are you willing to be the richest person in your family? Are you willing to say 'no' to people if they ask you for money? Are you willing to say 'yes' to people if they ask you for money? What if you had so much money that if people came and asked you for money, you could give it to them? What if you had so much money that if people came and asked you for money, you could say "Oh I'm so sorry, I wish you had asked me last week. I just put all my money into this particular project and I'm not going to be able to get any money from it for the next two years. Why don't you ask me in 2 years' time?" Everything that doesn't allow you to perceive, know, be and receive that, will you destroy and uncreate it all? Right and Wrong, Good and Bad, POD, POC, All 9, Shorts, Boys and Beyonds®

What energy, space and consciousness can your body and you be to have never enough money but always too much to spend? Everything that doesn't allow that, will you destroy and uncreate it all? Right and Wrong, Good and Bad, POD, POC, All 9, Shorts, Boys and Beyonds®

What physical actualization of a $100 million are you now capable of generating, creating and instituting? Everything that doesn't allow that to show up times godzillion will you destroy and uncreate it all? Right and Wrong, Good and Bad, POD, POC, All 9, Shorts, Boys and Beyonds®

What generative capacity for instant solidification of the elemental into reality by request of the quantum entanglements will send us more life, more living, more money, more fun and more of everything than you ever had before are you now capable of generating, creating and instituting? Everything that doesn't allow that to show up times godzillion will you destroy and uncreate it all? Right and Wrong, Good and Bad, POD, POC, All 9, Shorts, Boys and Beyonds®

Many of you think that money and wealth is being able to pay your bills rather than always having not enough money and too much to spend.

What can you be or do different today to change your financial reality right away? What can you be or do different today to bring in hundreds of thousands of dollars right away? Everything that doesn't allow that to show up with total ease, joy and glory, will you destroy and uncreate it all? Right and Wrong, Good and Bad, POD, POC, All 9, Shorts, Boys and Beyonds®

You also have to be willing to use money to create more money. How do you play with money to make more money right away? What are you capable of that you are not aware of? Everything that doesn't allow you to perceive, know, be and receive that, destroy and uncreate it all. Right and Wrong, Good and Bad, POD, POC, All 9, Shorts, Boys and Beyonds®

Play with that and see what shows up in your reality.

Caller: I still have this thing about going in the past about how I used to have more clients than right now. The awareness I received about that was that having too many clients, I get overwhelmed. Actually my boyfriend gets overwhelmed.

Nilofer: Everywhere that you've bought into your boyfriend's points of view and locked them in place in your life, your living, your body, your reality and your future, will you destroy and uncreate it all? Right and Wrong, Good and Bad, POD, POC, All 9, Shorts, Boys and Beyonds®

One of the things that I became aware of, looking at the small class sizes that I was creating is I had a point of view that my body could not handle that. I started asking my body to contribute to that. I'm willing to ask for contribution from my body. What if you were willing to ask for contribution from your boyfriend? You could say, "Honey, do you know, I am so grateful to you? You are such a contribution to my money flows. Would you contribute your energy to my money flows?" It's about him contributing energy to that.

Have you ever had this experience where you go into a shop or a restaurant, which is empty, and when you are there for a few minutes, it just starts to fill up? You are just contributing energy to that shop or that restaurant, and you are contributing to their money flows.

You can actually ask the people in your life to contribute to your money flows. If you ask your boyfriend, don't say, "so that more clients show up." Just ask him to contribute energy to your money flows.

He may have a point of view about you having too many clients. You don't want to trigger that. If you ask him to contribute energy to your money flows, he will be happy to. Also if you have kids, how about asking your kids to contribute energy to your business and your money flows?

The kids just get it like that. They will just know. They will just start contributing energy. When your kids ask you for something, and they ask, "Buy me this and buy me that?" I always tell my kids to think "How can I create this? What would it take for me to create it?" It sets them up into the energy of creating. The other thing is, I ask them "Can you contribute energy to my money flows, so I can make so much more money, so I can buy that thing?"

Caller: So do you just ask them to contribute energy? It's not like they have to do something about it, right?

Nilofer: We all have the capacity to contribute all the time. Yet, we never ask for things to contribute to us. Ask for contribution from everything in your home. Ask your home to contribute to your money flows. When you are actually buying things, ask them, "If I buy you, will you make me money?" You are giving it a job.

You are buying a shirt; for example, ask it, "If I buy you, will you make me money?" You are giving the molecules of this shirt the job of making you money. They are actually contributing to your money flows.

You can ask your business to contribute to you. You can ask your money and your bank account to contribute to you. You can ask your credit cards to contribute to you. You can ask your wallet to contribute to you. Everything can become a contribution when you are willing to ask for it. The contribution is always like a gifting and receiving.

You're going to be talking to everything around the house! That's what communion is. When you are in conversation with every molecule in the universe and every molecule talks to you, tells you what's going on.

One of the things my son does is he waters the plants in our home. I know the days when he has not watered the plants because they are screaming at me! "You have to give us water now! It's hot here! We need water now!" I just know the days. I'll look at the pot. I'll see that it's all dried up and he has forgotten to give it water. When you start pushing your barriers down and become willing to actually receive from everything and anything, that's what actually starts to show up for you in your life.

Even when you have a Bars class, just ask the class to contribute to you. You have to be willing to receive everything. Receiving is not only to do with how much money or material things you have, receiving is to do with awareness. What awareness is that class contributing to you? Then you use your energy flows to create the money flows.

Get the energy of the bars class in front of you and start pulling energy from all over the universe into that class. Then you send out trickles of energy to all the people who would like to attend that class and don't even know it. Ask the class to equalize the energy flow when those people have found it. Then you can also ask, "Class, who would you like to have as participants? Which bodies would you like to have?" You have to be willing to ask for bodies in your class, preferably bodies willing to pay for the class.

If you are asking for people, instead of asking for bodies, to show up; then there could be a lot of entities in your class. Ask, "What would it take to have more bodies, who will pay me, show up in my class?"

What energy, space and consciousness can your body and you be to have bigger and bigger classes with more bodies who pay for the class showing up with total ease, joy and glory for all eternity? Everything that doesn't allow that, destroy and uncreate it all. Right and Wrong, Good and Bad, POD, POC, All 9, Shorts, Boys and Beyonds®

ACCESS YOUR KNOWING & CREATE THE FUTURE YOU REALLY DESIRE

With Special Guest: Jonas Svensson at
http://www.moneycirclebook.com

CHAPTER EIGHT

CREATING FOR THE FUTURE

"What can you be or do different today to create money for you now and in the future right away?"

We all have had this experience of living from one paycheck to the other. You have the money for something and once that thing gets done, then you are again waiting for your next paycheck. Or if you are into creating classes, then you are creating for the class that you have right now, you put in all the efforts for that and get in the students for that, and then for the next class you have to put in that effort all over again.

So when you are doing that, you are actually only looking at the now. You are not creating for the future. You have to be willing to create for the now and the future.

You are working, working, working to create the money to pay your rent. Once you have the money to pay your rent, you stop doing anything, creating stuff. Until, again, you realize that "Oh my God, I have to pay the rent this month!" Again you start working towards creating that. So that way, you are creating for the now.

"What can you be or do different today to create money for you now and in the future right away?"

The other question you could ask is "What can you add to your life today to create money for you now and in the future right away?"

This could be to do with money. This could be to do with creating classes. This could be with creating a business. It could be with everything.

What creation are you using to invoke and perpetrate the functioning from the power of the now, as opposed to the power of the future you are choosing? Everything that is times godzillion will you destroy and uncreate it all? Right and Wrong, Good and Bad, POD, POC, All 9, Shorts, Boys and Beyonds®

So for your home-play for the next 7 days, you might want to run this clearing 30 times a day for the next 7 days. Also, use the 2 questions. What that will do is start putting you into this space of actually functioning from the now, as well as from the future.

As you start creating your life for the now and the future, you will never be at a place of "Oh my God, I don't have money anymore."

Let's compare the power of the future to the power of the now. This is the place that we are continuously in. At the beginning of the month, we are in this mode of creating money. Once we've kind of created enough money to have what we require, we stop creating. Then we repeat the same cycle over and over and over again the next month. Start creating for now and in the future.

What energy, space and consciousness can your body and you be to create money for you now and in the future with total ease, joy and glory? Everything that doesn't allow it, destroy and uncreate it all. Right and Wrong, Good and Bad, POD, POC, All 9, Shorts, Boys and Beyonds®

You have to have an awareness of the future, and you have to continuously be creating for the future. You can do clearings till kingdom comes, but if you don't take action along with it; you are not going to create anything. You have to use the tools, and you also have to take action along with it.

Gary spoke about his daughter. She went to him and said "Daddy, I've been using all the tools for 15 days. I have not created any money or any clients in my business." So he asked her "What did you do?" She said "Nothing." You have to do.

You have to do. These tools will get you to the point to which you will start to have possibilities show up in your life. When possibilities show up in your life, you have to be willing to take action. You have to be willing to do something which is going to create money for you.

Gary says that if you are a whore or a prostitute, you actually have to wear a short skirt, be willing to stand at the end of the street and solicit for trade, after having done all your clearings.

One of the things that I have found works very well for me is I will look at the different components of my business. There's a part of my business in which I'm doing my classes. There's another part of my business in which I do all my online stuff. I look at all of it and I ask, "What can I create today which is going to be fun for me? What can I create today which is going to be easy for me?" What happens is something or the other starts popping for me. I start taking action on that particular thing. The moment I take action, it just gets created. Then I start seeing other places that I can take action on. I start taking action on all those little places. Very soon I've got this whole host of things going on and money is coming in from one source or the other.

When you have multiple streams of income opening up for you, you are never going to obsess on "Oh my God, I'm doing this, this is not working out and money is not coming in."

Anything you have done to put all the eggs in one basket, will you destroy and uncreate it all? Right and Wrong, Good and Bad, POD, POC, All 9, Shorts, Boys and Beyonds®

What have you made so vital about possessing only one source of income that you would cut off all of your money flows in order to have it? Everything that doesn't allow that times godzillion, will you destroy and uncreate it all? Right and Wrong, Good and Bad, POD, POC, All 9, Shorts, Boys and Beyonds®

Caller: When I heard all Access people saying "money is just a choice," it felt so bizarre that I am not getting it. I need your facilitation today to have fun with money, saving money, shifting money, etc., doing all sorts of fun things even if they are not things with money. I don't remember when I last bought something just because I liked it. I've been buying things only on need and must have basis. I would like to change that. I'm using your tips and tools, but right now I cannot say that X amount showed up out of nowhere. Something in me is still not open to have money for just fun. This category has not been in my life. I literally have created this category, but till now it's still empty. Please help to change this.

Nilofer: Look at the money that you have. How much can you actually take out from that to play with? Put that money in your "fun with money" account. It could be as small as $5 or anything which is not going to break your bank, while also being expansive for you. Do this and you will be able to have it. Take that amount of money, look at it and say, "So, money, what can I do today to have fun with you right away?" Something will show up. Have fun with that money. It's like building a muscle. Initially when you start doing it, you have to do it very, very consciously. Slowly you are going to have more and more and more fun with money.

Create that "fun with money" account and start playing with it. Spend it on things which are really fun for you. Spend it on things that will expand your life, which will contribute to you. It will make you feel good. Pretty soon that fun is going to kind of buildup, and you will have fun with money.

CONTRIBUTING ENERGY

Caller: I forgot to tell you about a few changes. I have been following the summit for the third time now. Never had that heart to ask a question, but this time I did that with my heart beating so fast and loud. Now I am comfortable to ask questions. Thank you for that. I'm opening up so energetically.

Nilofer: How does it get any better than that?® It's awesome that you are in a place where you are willing to step out of your comfort zone, no matter what your comfort zone is. Just taking that one little step matters. It could be the first time you are just saying "Hi" on the call. That's what it takes. Have fun with that.

Caller: I do not yet have a story to share, but I would like to do so when I have a story. Can I have a 1-2-3 and a 1-2-3-4 for my money situation to shift right away?

Nilofer: A 1-2-3 is to change things in the past and the now. A 1-2-3-4 is to change the solidified futures about money. Put your awareness to your money situation. Now hold out your hands wide and start building up the energy in your hands. Then at the count of 3, you will flick that energy with total force onto your money situation.

Hold out your hands, then:
1. Build up the energy in your hands.
2. Build up more and more and more energy.
3. Flick all the built up energy, like a lightning bolt, onto your money situation.

Once again, 1-2-3, 1-2-3, 1-2-3, 1-2-3, 1-2-3.

Perceive the solidified futures that you have created and the contractions you have created around money, then do a 1-2-3-4 on it.

For the next one week, play with this tool. What if you could wake up in the morning, just perceive your money situation, then do ten 1-2-3s and ten 1-2-3-4s on your money situation? Notice what doing this starts to create for you. After three days, on the fourth day or maybe the fifth day, when you perceive the energy of your money situation, it will have completely changed for you.

SELLING PROPERTY

Caller: I have a house that has been on the market for sale for quite a while that hasn't sold yet. I have dropped the price of the house several times. I have a tenant and her family living there. I am receiving some income from it. She is getting assistance from the government to help pay her rent and has not been paying her share of the rent for over a year now. I'd like some help with getting my house sold, my tenant paying her part of the rent and the taxes paid for the house. Thank you.

Nilofer: Get the energy of the house and place it in front of you. Now start pulling in energy from all over the universe into that energy of the house. Keep pulling more energy until you feel your heart expand. Once that happens, send out trickles of energy to everyone who is looking to buy your house and doesn't even know it. Then ask the house to equalize the energy once it has found the person(s) it would like to own. We don't own houses or objects; actually they own us because we are the ones who go to work to get the money to pay for them. The house owns you. Send out trickles of energy. Then tell your house that when it finds the person(s) it would like to own, equalize the energy flow. Your house will get sold.

The other thing you have to do is ask the house "How much would you like to be sold for?" Sometimes, you might decide on a lower price. Yet, what if the house wants to be sold for a higher price? Ask the house how much it would like to be sold for. Put that price up on the market, and use these energy pulls to create a buyer. Do this every single day.

To get your client to pay her part of the rent, you use the energy pull. Pull energy through your client, from the universe, through your client to you and pull it through your whole body. Pull massive amounts of energy from your tenant. Pull massive amounts of energy, and don't stop it at your body. Fill your body and allow it to flow out. After you pull massive amounts of energy from your client, send trickles of energy to her. Basically what this will do is that she will just not be able to get you out of her head. She *will* pay you.

To get the taxes paid for the house, you have to actually look at exactly how much the tax is for the house. Then go to question "What would it take for me to pay the tax with total ease?" If you know the amount of money for the tax, then ask "What would it take for me to pay X amount of money with total ease?" You also have to be willing to look at what work you can do to create the money or how many hours you need to work to create that extra money.

Like I said before, you can use the tools until kingdom comes. If you don't go out and take action for it, nothing is going to show up. You have to be willing to see what action(s) you can take to have that thing show up. Maybe you need to go and do a job, whatever is available to you. Look at how much that job pays you. Look at the amount of money you have to pay and how many hours you need to work at that job to create that money.

It's not that you are going to this desperation, "Oh my God, I need to do this." It's that you have to demonstrate to the universe that you are willing to take any action it takes to create that. Once you start taking any action, even one small step of you venturing out to give a job interview, the universe will start to give you different possibilities. You might just go for an interview, meet someone over there and end up talking to them. They might tell you about this other available job. You have to just be willing to take any action. Use the tool. Take action. Both are required to create change.

Caller: What I feel about money is that I'm tired of wishing for it, chasing it, doing everything I know to create it and I'm sick of running behind it. It makes me feel like a desperate prostitute for wanting to have it. Why am I the one who money refuses to come to and stay with? I can't have more than 575 dirhams at one time. That's the feeling in me somehow. Can you dissolve that feeling and give some clearing to increase my receiving level?

Nilofer: "Why am I the one who money refuses to come to and stay in?" is not a question. It's actually energetically a conclusion with a question mark attached to it.

Ask "What can I be or do different today to change this right away?" We are continuously in this judgment that what we are asking for is not showing up.

What have you made so vital about totally possessing the struggle of failure, like all humans, that keep success always as failure? Everything that is times godzillion will you destroy and uncreate it all? Right and Wrong, Good and Bad, POD, POC, All 9, Shorts, Boys and Beyonds®

We look at whatever is showing up in our life and go to judgment that something is wrong there. What if there is nothing wrong there? What if making it wrong was only your judgment? No matter what shows up in your life, even if it is 1 dirham (Dirham is the currency on the United Arab Emirates, where the author lives) showing up, what if you would ask "How does it get any better than this?" What will it take for ten times this to show up?" If you just have 575 dirhams showing up at one time, look at it and ask, "What's right about this that I'm not getting? What else is possible here that I haven't yet considered?"
We have this insidious need to continuously go into conclusion and judgment, instead of question. What if you would actually go to question all the time? Sometimes you may need to say the question like a hundred million times before things will start to shift for you. What if you could be the demand "I don't care what it takes, but this is going to change.

What would it take for something totally different to show up?" You have to be willing to change. Not change in the way that you would like it to change, but something totally different. It's not differently, but something totally different to show up.

When you say "I don't care what has to happen, something has to change here," you are not making this demand of the universe. You are actually making a demand of yourself to change whatever energy you are being which is creating this, so that something different can show up. If you look at this truthfully, there is an energy you are either being or not being which is creating whatever it is that is showing up in your life. So, demand "I don't care what it takes, but this has to change. And this has to change right now." Then ask, "What can I be or do different today to get this right away?"

What have you made so vital about having a ceiling on your receiving that you would cut off your money flows in order to have it? Everything that is times godzillion will you destroy and uncreate it all? Right and Wrong, Good and Bad, POD, POC, All 9, Shorts, Boys and Beyonds®

What are you judging as not successful that actually would create you as being more successful? Everything that is times godzillion will you destroy and uncreate it all? Right and Wrong, Good and Bad, POD, POC, All 9, Shorts, Boys and Beyonds®

Another clearing you can run: What would it take for me to get more money all the time? Everything that doesn't allow it, destroy and uncreate it all. Right and Wrong, Good and Bad, POD, POC, All 9, Shorts, Boys and Beyonds®

Caller: I have been using the questions and tools you provide, but I can't stop feeling tight on money. The tightness makes me feel trapped, barely surviving. I know I am the creator in my life, but clearly I keep creating the tightness and dependency no matter how many questions I ask. Please help me.

Nilofer: Ask the questions: "What is this? What do I do with it? Can I change it? How can I change it?"

Basically, it is just an energy you have labelled as tightness. Wherever you have labelled any energy as tightness or anything else destroy and uncreate it all. Right and Wrong, Good and Bad, POD, POC, All 9, Shorts, Boys and Beyonds®

Take that energy and contribute it to your money flows. Notice what happens. Does it expand or does it contract? It expands. Now take that energy and contribute it to your bank account. Then you have this expansion which happens. When you stop labeling something, it becomes available as free energy to you. You can take that energy and contribute it to different areas of your life. Contribution is always simultaneity of gifting and receiving. As you gift that energy, it expands. Then you have more and more and more energy, which is available for you to use it in different areas of your life.

Look at your credit card and contribute that energy to your credit card. Feel that expansion. It's not that you are increasing your credit card debt; it's actually reducing your credit card debt by contributing your energy there. Never refer to it as 'debt'. Refer to debt as a past expenditure. All the other places of money you have in your life like your bank account, your PayPal™ account, any kind of savings and bonds that you have; contribute that energy there and just allow it to expand. The next time you go to this place of perceiving any energy, what if you were to destroy and uncreate all the labels you have created for it. Then use that energy and contribute it to different areas of your life?

Contribute that energy to your body. I interviewed Donnielle Carter. We were talking about bodies and money. She said that most of the things we do with money in this reality have to do with providing things for our body. You need money to pay rent because you require a house to live in, to buy the food to eat, to buy air tickets… So everywhere you are taking that money, it is to do with gifting to your body. What if you were to ask for contribution from your body to your money flows?

Ask, "Hey body, would you contribute energy to increasing my money flows?" Your body is really happy to do that. Ask for the contribution from your body. The next time you would like to buy anything, ask your body "Hey body, would you like this? Would you contribute energy to having this? Body, what would it take for us to have this?"

Include your body in all the things that involve your body and ask for its contribution.

Caller: I just don't seem to enjoy my money or his. I keep asking "Money, how much fun can we have today?" but I don't really enjoy it. It feels as if I'm taking someone's share, as if I really don't have any share of money for me. Please help. I just cannot order in a restaurant. I eat whatever someone orders. I really would like to change this. I really would like to have more freedom and choice with money.

Nilofer: Say this 3 times: "I really don't have any share of money for me." All the SHICCUUUU (**S**ecret, **H**idden, **I**nvisible, **C**overt, **U**nseen, **U**nsaid, **U**ndisclosed, **U**nacknowledged) implants and explants keeping all of that in place destroy and uncreate it all. Right and Wrong, Good and Bad, POD, POC, All 9, Shorts, Boys and Beyonds®

You also have to go take action. The next time you go to a restaurant order a dish for you, no matter how small it is. Just choose the things that make you step out of your comfort zone. You do the clearings, you use the tools and then you take action.

Caller: On the last call you suggested that someone ask their boyfriend if he would contribute his energy to her business. I have a business. I'm the sole support of my boyfriend and myself. I asked him if he would contribute energy to the business, and he got angry. What should I do? Thanks.

Nilofer: Ask him what he misidentified and misapplied as contributing energy to your business. Did he go to a place of judgement that you were asking him to work for the business or were you judging him for not giving money or anything like that? It looks like it created some kind of funky energy over there. Everything that is, times godzillion will you destroy and uncreate it all? Right and Wrong, Good and Bad, POD, POC, All 9, Shorts, Boys and Beyonds®

If someone is not even willing to contribute energy to your business, then what is the value of that person in your life? Energy is something which is available to all of us and it is something with which we can actually contribute to all the people in our life. We can use it to contribute to the whole planet. You have to look at what that's creating for you.

Have a conversation with him. He may have some points of view around this. You don't need to physically ask a person to contribute energy to the business. You can actually just silently ask people to contribute energy to the business. I know this works really, really well. So you could think about him and go, "What contribution can you be to my business and my money flows?" It's almost like the moment you ask, you will receive that energy. You also have to acknowledge the places where he is actually being a contribution to your money flows and your business just by being in your life.

Just be grateful for that energy and have a conversation. Don't be in this energy of having him be angry at you. When someone is angry at you, your money flows decrease.

HAVING FUN YET?

YOU WILL when you sign up for the interviews! To get more tips, strategies, tools and ideas that can help you be totally present, totally aware and be willing to receive the infinite intensity of the infinite colors of infinite possibilities Visit
http://www.moneycirclebook.com

CHAPTER NINE

FOUR TOOLS

"Never give up, never give in, never quit" ~ Gary Douglas

The tools I share here will give you those breakthroughs that you require to change not only your money situation, but any other situation in your life.

FIRST TOOL – NEVER TAKE NO

The first thing is something I heard Gary Douglas, the founder of Access Consciousness®, say in one of the classes I attended with him. What he said was "I never take 'no' as an answer to anything." He went on to say that no matter what is going on, he never takes 'no' for an answer. He keeps creating and creating and creating. What if you never take 'no' for an answer? No matter how much you know, you are working towards it. No matter if it is not happening at the moment, if you never took 'no' for an answer, I wonder what that would change in your universe?

I'd like to like share a little story here. As I write this, just yesterday one of my friends called me. She has been going through a challenging time in her relationship with her husband. They are thinking about separating and getting divorced. So one of the things her husband did was change the code for the safe in which they keep all their documents. She has some really important documents inside that safe that she wanted to retrieve. He was not willing to give her the new code.

She has been playing around with the tools of Access Consciousness®. What she did was go into question. She just asked "What if I could guess the code for the safe?" She asked this question for a few days with the energy of play. She had no expectations. It's just been like she's been playing with it.

She said "So, yesterday, as I was driving, I just happened to see the number on the plate of the car we have." It just popped into her head that maybe that could be the code to the safe. She went home, punched in that number and the safe opened. This is an example of not being willing to take 'no' for an answer.

So no matter what it is, what if you were not willing to take "no" as an answer? What if you knew that something else was always possible?

SECOND TOOL - DEMAND

The second thing is that all those things you think are not changing that you just look at it and you just feel depressed or maybe feel this sense of no hope about, what if you were to look at those things and be a demand? Being a demand is not about demanding from the universe. You know? "Universe, you will have to give me this." The demand is actually from you.

So what energy, space and consciousness do you have to be or do different for that situation to change for you? Now, most of the time we want things to change a little and only in the way that we want it to change. What if you are willing for it to change in whatever way it could change? So if you become this energy of demand: no matter what it takes, no matter how long it takes, no matter what I have to do, no matter what I have to lose, I am going to make sure that this changes? What energy can I be or do different to make sure that this changes? When you are willing to be a demand, then that thing will totally, definitely change for you. That's the second thing.

THIRD TOOL – NO CONCLUSIONS AND JUDGEMENTS

The third thing is conclusions and judgments. So most of the time we ask for change to show up while having all these conclusions and judgments in place about how that change has to show up and when. It's almost like you were to plant a seed, then you go and water the seed, and every day you are digging the soil to check if the seed has grown. That's what conclusions and judgments do. So if you dig the seed every single day, is the seed ever going to grow? So conclusions and judgments are the two things which will kill whatever you are asking for right away.

In one of the Access Consciousness® classes, I heard Gary say that "conclusion and judgment are the law of attraction. So, whatever you conclude or whatever you judge, you are making sure that you are attracting that into your life." Now is that really what you would like to do?

What if instead of conclusion or judgment, you go to question "What would it take for this to show up?" Even if you have these conclusions and judgments show up, you can ask "What would it take to make these conclusions and judgments go away?" Then destroy and uncreate times godzillion all those conclusions and judgments.

No matter what is going on, what if you were to keep going to question? I know this can be a little challenging – maybe the hardest thing you've ever done. (Yet, what would it take for it to be ease, joy and glory?) Going to question is just like a muscle. So, every time you find yourself going into conclusion or judgment, you can destroy and uncreate it or you could say "Oh I'm going into conclusion and judgment. Never mind. What else can I choose here? What else is possible here?" So it is like a muscle that you have to build and exercise. You have to keep practicing it all the time.

FOURTH TOOL – NO VESTED INTEREST

The fourth thing is whatever you are asking for; don't have a vested interest in the outcome. If you have a vested interest, if you are projecting onto it, if you have expectations from it, what's going to happen is you are going to kill it off again. So every day when you look at what you are asking for, destroy and uncreate all your projections, expectations, separations, rejections and judgments about that project or about that thing you are asking for, now and in the future. Destroy and uncreate all the vested interests you have. You are destroying and un-creating the project so that it can show up way greater than you could never have imagined. Only by destroying and un-creating it are you allowing it to create itself way greater than what you could have imagined.

Let me repeat the four things again here:
1. Never take 'no'
2. Be a demand. The demand is not from the universe. The demand is from you.
3. No conclusions and judgments.
4. No vested interest.

What energy, space and consciousness can you be or do different for having whatever it is that you are asking for to show up? Destroy and uncreate all your judgments and conclusions and keep going to question. Keep asking "What else is possible?" What else is possible that I haven't even considered?"

Every day destroy and uncreate that whole project. Destroy and uncreate all your projections, expectations, separations, rejections and judgments around it.

Just today in the morning, when I woke up, I actually sat down and made a list. I said to myself "you know, what are all those things which I think are never going to change in my life?" I actually wrote those things. As

I was looking at each one of those things, I applied all these four points that I've just shared with you here. As I was applying the 4 points to each one of those things, I could see that everything is possible and everything can be changed. So that's the last little tip I would like to leave you with. Write down all those things you think are never ever going to change and apply this 4-step process to it. Then notice what shows up.

I used the four tools above and had such a gift show up after that. It was phenomenal. I have this PayPal™ account, which I opened up in some other country so I could accept credit card payments online. I opened up that account not knowing that I needed to verify that account before I could withdraw money from the account. I had a whole bunch of money in that account. When I actually started to send the money somewhere, I realized that the account was not verified. So, I could not send out the money from there. I've been doing my best to open that up, so I could use the money from that account. No matter what I tried, it wasn't working. However, I did use the tool, "What else is possible?®" I have been continuously in that question. "What else is possible here?®"

When I would look at that account this energy would show up, "No matter what, this is not going to change." I would say "I'm not buying into that. What else is possible here?® I don't care how much time it takes, I don't care when it has to show up, but this thing is going to open up for me."

I wrote down these 4 tools. The next day, by mistake, I tried to pay $1 from that account. It got paid. I realized it only the next day. So to test it, I did a second payment. Then I did a third payment, all through my mobile app. When I opened up the account, it was still unverified. However, there was a little notification that said, "Your sending limit has been removed." What that means is that I can send the money from there to anyone I want to, anywhere, via PayPal™. How does it get any better than that?®

This is the power of never taking 'no' in action. Just start working with the tools. Don't go to conclusions. Don't go to judgments. If you go to that, just destroy and uncreate it all. Just create more and more.

ARE YOU MIMICKING YOUR FAMILY?

Caller: I have been running the clearings every day and I have moved into action. Having a second full-time job has given me a cushion and created more ease with paying my monthly bills. Working two jobs is not total ease. I'm in action and I know that is what is required. I am being different. However, I'm running so much now. I find myself only stopping to wash clothes, to get to work and put gas in my car. This energy is familiar to me as it is the energy of struggle. I can't have space to live my life, be me and have the money to fund it at the same time. I'm asking how can I out-create this? What energy, space and consciousness can me and my body be or do different to change this? Working all the time is not fun for me. I'm asking for clarity, also, on if this is the right choice for me now? Some days I feel as if I am a harsh task-master overriding my body and forcing non-stop work. I said to my body, "If you stop working, you won't have food, shelter, clothing, health or relationship." I'm also asking what stupidity am I using to create this stupidity I'm choosing. These energies are familiar and valued in my family. I've been perpetuating these insanities for many years. Any awareness on how to bust this up will be appreciated. Thank you.

Nilofer: What creation are you using to invoke and perpetrate the biomimetic and biomimetric mimicry of your family's pain, pathways and realities about work are you choosing? Everything that is times godzillion will you destroy and uncreate it all? Right and Wrong, Good and Bad, POD, POC, All 9, Shorts, Boys and Beyonds®

You are continuously mimicking your family's realities around money. Run this process 30 times a day for the next at least 90 days. Things will start to shift and change for you, as you stop mimicking your family's reality. You will start to have your own reality with money show up, which is a question you can go to. "What would I like to create my monetary reality as?" Get the energy of it and start creating beyond that energy.

The other thing you said is you are forcing stuff on your body. How about asking for your body's contribution? You can ask, "Hey body, what can you contribute to my money situation? How can this be ease for me?"

In the last month I have been actually facilitating a lot of classes. Also, most of these classes are an hour drive from my home. By the time I was in the third class, I had this energy of tiredness in my body show up. I started asking my body, "Body, what would it take for you to contribute to this?" and "How can this be ease for us? How can we make this easier on us?" I was in that question and my body actually started contributing to it. I started just experiencing this ease in my body. Then I had a class, which was scheduled after that, and my body was clear "We are not doing that class. That class is not going to be a contribution to us." It was such a clear awareness to me that I just chose not to do that class. I told myself "I'm not doing this now. I will reschedule the class to some other time."

You have to be willing to listen to what your body is saying. Maybe your body needs to do something else. Maybe it needs time to go out for a walk. Maybe you need time to just sleep in. So try taking time off one day in a week. Maybe you will enjoy a few hours just to sleep in or maybe have a nice bath or just go for a massage.

Just create something, which is going to be nurturing for your body. After that class was over, I had this whole day where I was just sitting in bed all day. I had some yummy books with me. All I did was just laze around in bed all day and read those books. It just created this ease in my universe. The next day, I was again up and about. I was doing work, creating and generating new things. Yet, it's like my body got that one day of rest and it was plugging in. Don't exclude your body. Include your body in creating money, because that is how you are creating the money to actually contribute to the body. Ask for your body's contribution to create money in your life.

Caller: My mother owns 2 companies. I am employed in both of them. I am interested in doing something with the second company that she is not so interested in. She lets me run it more or less my way. This company is situated in a beautiful house that is also owned by my mother. I had started my bars classes here, and I'm also very excited about that. I would also like to hold Access Consciousness® events here. However, I noticed that for some reason whenever I am hosting another facilitator there, no one even registers for the class, which I find interesting. To be more specific when there is a pre-introduction to the class, people sign up for it, but not for the actual class. What is going on here? What's right about this I'm not getting? Does it have something to do with my energies or is it something else? Can you help me with this and shed some light on the subject? I'm very grateful for your contribution. Thank you.

Nilofer: What do you know about this that will give you more clarity and ease with it? Everything that doesn't allow you to perceive, know, be and receive that, will you destroy and uncreate it all? Right and Wrong, Good and Bad, POD, POC, All 9, Shorts, Boys and Beyonds®

You can talk to your mother and ask her to contribute energy to it. When she starts contributing energy to it, she will actually be included in what you are doing.

How much is your point of view, "my mother is not interested in doing something with the second company," contributing to whatever is going on with your work? Everything that is will you destroy and uncreate it all? Right and Wrong, Good and Bad, POD, POC, All 9, Shorts, Boys and Beyonds®

The biggest thing that we miss out in this whole equation of creation is asking for the energetic contribution, and most people are contributing energy all the time.

I always give people this example: Have you ever had this experience of going to a restaurant or going into a shop, which was totally empty, and it just fills up in a short while when you are there? How much is it you actually contributing energy to the money flows of that place that allowed all these other customers to come in and start buying things there?

We all have this capacity of contributing energy. You are doing it all the time. When you actually ask people to contribute energy to it, they are just happy to contribute energy to it, which creates so much ease in our universe.

When you have two energies contributing to something, you will create way more than what you could have created before. Ask your mother to contribute energy to that business and to all the events that are happening there.

When hosting other facilitators, ask "If I choose this, what will the business be like in 5 years, 10 years, 15 years' time? If I don't choose this, what will the business be like in 5 years, 10 years, 15 years' time?" You have to, also, ask the question, "If I choose this, will you make me money?"

When you start asking that question to the class or to whichever class you have created to show up in that space, what happens is that you are giving this job to the class to actually create more money. You can also say, "If I choose this, will you create participants showing up? Will you create bodies showing up?" Sometimes when you ask for participants to show up, there are a lot of beings who show up who are not necessarily in bodies. So sometimes I like to ask my classes, if I choose this, will beings in bodies show up? Then that's what happens.

My point of view is that if it is in the same hometown as I am in, even if I am not having people show up for the class, I will do the class. Why? I have seen what an amazing contribution those people are and how much of a gift they are in the world. I also perceive how much I receive from the class when I am facilitating them.

The other thing is look at your business as an energy. If you start looking at the energy of your business and start perceiving where the energy is a little bit dense, you can do a 1-2-3 on that energy. Get the energy of your business and your money flows. Then on the count of 3, contribute energy to it. Hold up your hands and start building up the energy in your hand, 1-2-and-3. At the count of 3, flick energy at it like a thunderbolt.

Look at the solidified futures that you have created around your money flows and the solidified futures you have created around your business. Perceive the energy of it. Then do a 1-2-3-4 on all those solidified futures. Build up the energy in your hand and 1-2-3-4, 1-2-3-4, 1-2-3-4.

If you wake up in the morning and you do ten 1-2-3s and ten 1-2-3-4s on your money flows every single day, you will start to create a shift and change in your money flows. Play with that. Create a shift and change in your business, and then again, go into that question.

What energy, space and consciousness can my body and I be to change all this in totality right away for all eternity? Everything that doesn't allow this, destroy and uncreate it all. Right and Wrong, Good and Bad, POD, POC, All 9, Shorts, Boys and Beyonds®

When you want to create those classes which have 25 people showing up and they are not, instead of going to the judgment and conclusion of it, go to question. "What else is possible here I haven't even considered? What can I be or do different today to change this right away?" So many times I have found not going to questions like, "what will it take to create 25 people?" or whatever, and instead just going to the question, "what can I be or do different today to change this right away?" will create more. Why? You are willing to create a change in that right away, and things will start to shift and change for you.

Sometimes, what happens is that the place that you are asking for change may take time for that change to show up. Yet, you may start to see a change show up in a different place. I have these classes that I do in the country that I live in. In the summer I travel to India, and I have a class scheduled in India, as well. So I've been asking for questions to change the energy of the classes which are showing up here in the UAE. I'm using this question "what can I be or do different today to change this right away?" What is starting to show up is awarenesses of all the different things or all the different points of view I have, which are actually stopping people from showing up in my life. This is how I am uninviting people to show up in my classes.

Where are you uninviting people to show up in your classes? Everything that is will you destroy and uncreate it all? Right and Wrong, Good and Bad, POD, POC, All 9, Shorts, Boys and Beyonds®

I had interviewed Simone Milasas a couple of years ago. On that interview she shared to run this clearing every night, "Where have I uninvited money into my life today? Everything that is destroy and uncreate it all. Right and Wrong, Good and Bad, POD, POC, All 9, Shorts, Boys and Beyonds®"

I've been asking for change to show up in my classes in the UAE. What has started to happen is that the registrations are coming in for my class in India. You don't know where the energy is going, what you are actually creating when you choose to go to question, instead of conclusion.

Maybe the place that you are creating classes on may not show up there, but it may show up somewhere totally different. Are you willing to receive that? Are you willing to ask for that? Have no conclusions about how things are showing up and keep going to the question of what else is possible here? What can I be or do different today to change this right away?

The other thing I've noticed is that whenever I use my favorite question "What else is possible here?®" it's almost like I'm becoming aware of all the fixed points of view that I have which are stopping that thing from showing up in my life. As I keep using that question or be in that question, it's like I can perceive the point of view that I have. I can perceive how I'm letting go of that point of view.

All the fixed points of view you have, which are preventing whatever you are asking for to show up in your life, will you now destroy and uncreate it all? Right and Wrong, Good and Bad, POD, POC, All 9, Shorts, Boys and Beyonds®

What points of view are you using to create the limitations you are choosing? Everything that is times godzillion will you destroy and uncreate it all? Right and Wrong, Good and Bad, POD, POC, All 9, Shorts, Boys and Beyonds®

What points of view are you using to create the limitations around money you are choosing? Everything that is times godzillion will you destroy and uncreate it all? Right and Wrong, Good and Bad, POD, POC, All 9, Shorts, Boys and Beyonds®

What points of view are you using to create the limited classes or the minuscule classes you are choosing? Everything that is times godzillion will you destroy and uncreate it all? Right and Wrong, Good and Bad, POD, POC, All 9, Shorts, Boys and Beyonds®

I have a friend who is this amazing woman. She was telling me how she lives in India for 6 months in a year and lives in other places the other time. She goes to these places and creates money for herself. She loves the sea, so she created a house at a good price for herself living very near the sea. She would go to a coffee shop and run this clearing on herself. As she ran the clearing, she would start getting clients who booked sessions with her. She says "If I run this clearing for about 10-15 minutes, I will get at least one new client in a day. If I run this clearing for about 40-45 minutes, I have 3 or 4 new people showing up as my clients." How does it get any better than that? This is an amazing clearing to use.

What judgments are you using that are limiting your receiving of money and clients today? Everything that is, will you destroy and uncreate it all? Right and Wrong, Good and Bad, POD, POC, All 9, Shorts, Boys and Beyonds®

WHAT CAN YOU RECEIVE TODAY THAT YOU HAVE BEEN UNWILLING TO RECEIVE BEFORE?

Caller: Nilofer, I can't be on the call today, but I wanted to take the time to let you know I am so grateful for all the things you've shared in these 9 weeks. I'm listening to the series and I've been making money every day. Thank you. On this day I don't have a question, only gratefulness. And out of the tools, the one tool that I love the most is lowering my barriers.

Nilofer: That is my favorite tool, as well, lowering my barriers. I am just becoming so much more aware of how much receiving lowering my barriers is creating. For such a long time, I functioned from this place of 'ignorance is bliss' and 'Oh my God, it is so painful and so uncomfortable to know.' I mean it is great to know the good things in life, but I didn't want to know the bad and the ugly things in life, and ugly things about me. As I'm lowering my barriers to me, I'm receiving more and more of me—the good, the bad and the ugly—with no points of view. I can see how much potency I have, how much power I have, to start changing all the things which are bad and ugly about me with no point of view about it.

I'm totally in this place where, if I perceive something about me, I think "I'm so glad I can see this. Now what would it take for me to change it?" The question, "what would it take for me to change it," is not coming from a judgement. It's coming from an acknowledgement of who I am, and being willing to change it.

Just lower your barriers more and more.

What will you receive today that you have been unwilling to receive, that if you were to receive it would change your whole reality? Everything that doesn't allow you to perceive, know, be and receive that, will you destroy and uncreate it all? Right and Wrong, Good and Bad, POD, POC, All 9, Shorts, Boys and Beyonds®

What if you were willing to receive it no matter what it is? What if you were to receive the good, the bad and the ugly of you with no point of view? What contribution would that be in your life? Just lower your barriers to receiving you. Lower your barriers some more.

What are you unwilling to receive about you that if you received that would give you more you? Everything that doesn't allow you to perceive, know, be and receive that, will you destroy and uncreate it all? Right and Wrong, Good and Bad, POD, POC, All 9, Shorts, Boys and Beyonds®

Are you receiving your body or do you have your barriers up to your body? What if you could have them down and that vulnerability with your body, as well? Lower your barriers to your body.

What are you defending for or against your body that if you stopped defending for or against it would give you a communion with your body that would create everything you desire? Everything that doesn't allow that, will you destroy and uncreate it all? Right or Wrong, Good and Bad, POC and POD, All 9, Shorts, Boys and Beyonds.

What are you unwilling to receive about your body that if you received it, would change your whole reality about money and receiving? Everything that doesn't allow that, will you destroy and uncreate it all? Right and Wrong, Good and Bad, POD, POC, All 9, Shorts, Boys and Beyonds®

What have you made so vital about never receiving your body that is cutting off all your receiving? Everything that is will you destroy and uncreate it all? Right and Wrong, Good and Bad, POD, POC, All 9, Shorts, Boys and Beyonds®

What stupidity are you using to create the lack of receiving your body you are choosing? Everything that is times godzillion will you destroy and uncreate it all? Right and Wrong, Good and Bad, POD, POC, All 9, Shorts, Boys and Beyonds®

Perceive the energy of receiving your body and do a 1-2-3 on that. (10 times)

Look at all the solidified futures that you've created from not receiving your body, and do a 1-2-3-4 on that.(10 times)

How many judgments do you have about your body that doesn't allow you to receive our body? Everything that is times godzillion will you destroy and uncreate it all? Right and Wrong, Good and Bad, POD, POC, All 9, Shorts, Boys and Beyonds®

How much money would you receive if you were to receive your body in totality today? Everything that doesn't allow you to perceive, know, be and receive that, will you destroy and uncreate it all? Right and Wrong, Good and Bad, POD, POC, All 9, Shorts, Boys and Beyonds®

What judgments of bodies are you using to create the lack of money you are choosing? Everything that is times godzillion will you destroy and uncreate it all? Right and Wrong, Good and Bad, POD, POC, All 9, Shorts, Boys and Beyonds®

CONTRIBUTIONS FOR YOUR BUSINESS

Caller: I have a question. I'm starting a new career and I'm wondering what is stopping me from moving forward quickly. I've been asking myself this. Part of it is like it's about building relationships and making connections with people. I'm not sure what questions to ask that will facilitate making connections and communicating with people with ease. It's a business. So my goal is to meet new clients and offer to just connect with my friends and family, and just like share my business with them. Show them what it is.

Nilofer: If you are starting a business and want to make connections for the business, you just connect to your friends and family. Call up everyone you know and ask them about what's going on in their life. When they ask you what you are doing, then you tell them about your business. Then ask "Do you know anyone who could benefit from this?" or "Can you help with this?" or "Can you refer people to me who could benefit from this?"

This is what Gary says, "If you were to make 3 phone calls every single day and this is all that you did, pretty soon you would actually start filling up your business. Pretty soon you would start to have clients showing up."

It's like calling people without an agenda to make something happen. It's just to check in. When you have an agenda, people know it as you talk. It's almost like you are projecting it at them, and then they have to fight you for it.

When you are calling it an agenda, mentally you have this conversation going "Oh my God, I'm calling up this person and I need to sign him up as a client." That itself becomes a limitation which will stop you. Yet, if you are picking up the phone to talk to three people, that's fun, isn't it? You could talk to 3 people. You could just talk and go "Hey, what's going on with you?" Then they'll tell you whatever is going on with them. If they remember to ask you what's going on with you, you could say "Hey, I'm starting this new business where I offer these anti-ageing facelift sessions to people and it's just like it's almost like getting a facial but it's much more permanent. It'll make a person look younger, and can you help me by referring people to me?"

When you go to "Can you help me by referring someone else?" they don't get that you are trolling for clients or anything from them, which they have to fight you for. They will just get that energy of "I could help. Sure I know people who are interested in this thing." Then you can offer to send your business cards or your flyers or whatever. They are happy to pass it on to people. Who knows, they might just want to join in as well. This is just like a little technique that you are using to bypass their resistance.

Don't have a point of view about the time limit for this. Most of the people I've seen would like something to show up, and then they have a point of view about it. After two months they'll suddenly go "Oh my God, I'm doing this and nothing is working." The moment you go to this place of "nothing is working," nothing will work, because you have created a conclusion about it.

What if you were to just be in the question all the time? What else is possible? If that thing you are looking to create, if it's not yet time for it to show up, something else will show up in the universe, which you will be able to create a lot from. Going to question, instead of conclusion, will start to create your business in a way you never expected it to.

I would absolutely love to know what has been shifting and changing in your life with regards to money and with regards to receiving. So please do write in. How much more fun can you have? What would it take for you to make thousands of dollars from everything you do every day?

WHO IS NILOFER SAFDAR?

Nilofer Safdar is a two times bestselling author of the books, Cracking the Client Attraction Code and The Colors Of Now. She teaches people how to write, be published and become a bestselling author in 90 days, even if they have never written before (or think they can never write). She is a strong advocate of getting a book published. Her pet peeve is to educate people on why everyone must write a book.

She is a Certified Access Consciousness Facilitator, CFMW. Nilofer helps people change their reality to generate and create a life they desire and require. Her target is to generate a life that is joyful and expansive for everybody she touches.

Nilofer is also a Right Relationship For You Facilitator and a Right Voice For You Facilitator.

Nilofer is a Life Coach, Money Mastery Coach, Public Speaking Coach, Relationship Coach, and Weight Loss and Anti-Aging Expert.

She is the host of a TV show which aired on JIA News in India, *The Nilofer Show*.

She is the host of the First online radio show in the Middle East, *The Healthy Living Dubai Show*. She interviews Speakers, Coaches and Natural Healers from the Middle East, which empowers the listeners to create everything they desire in life.

She is also the host of the telesummit, Illusion to Illumination Summit. She has interviewed more than 150 Luminaries, Change Agents and Best Selling Authors from around the world, including Peggy Phoenix Dubro, the originator of the EMF Balancing Technique, and Gary Douglas, the founder of Access Consciousness®.

She regularly contributes articles to the publication, *Tempo Planet*.

To contact Nilofer for further information about her books, audios, newsletters, workshops & training programs, and consultancy or to schedule her for a presentation, please write to:

nilofer@illusiontoilluminationsummit.com

Websites are –
www.illusiontoilluminationsummit.com
www.healthylivingdubai.com
www.nilofersafdar.com
www.walkinginbalance.net

BOOKS BY NILOFER

More Books By Nilofer Safdar
Books By Nilofer – http://www.nilofersbooks.com

Cracking The Client Attraction Code - #1 Bestseller
By Carla McNeil & Nilofer Safdar
http://www.crackingtheclientattractioncode.com

The Colors Of Now - #1 Bestseller
By Nilofer Safdar
http://www.thecolorsofnow.com

Money Circle
By Nilofer Safdar
http://moneycirclebook.com

Where Is My Doorway To Possibilities
By Nilofer Safdar
http://www.whereismydoorwaytopossibilities.com

Transformations
By Nilofer Safdar
http://www.thetransformationsbook.com

The Magic Of Being
By Nilofer Safdar
http://www.magicofbeing.com

Coming Soon
Choice The Liberator
By Nilofer Safdar

Creation From Joy
By Nilofer Safdar

30 Days Business Bootcamp
By Aditi Surti & Nilofer Safdar

WHAT NEXT?

All the tools and techniques from this book are from the body of work called Access Consciousness®.

If you haven't already, I would highly recommend you start with the Access Consciousness® Core Classes – Bars & Foundation.

Nilofer can facilitate each of these classes and is happy to travel to facilitate them.

You can find more information on these classes at www.accessconsciousness.com

MORE FROM NILOFER SAFDAR

Private Coaching

Symphony Of Possibilities

Book Creation (Writing, Publishing, Bestseller Ranking)

Bars

Body Work

Relationship Coaching (Right Relationship For You)

Public Speaking & Personality Development (Right Voice For You)

Business Coaching

Phases I – XIII of EMF Balancing Technique

SESSIONS WITH NILOFER (PHONE/In Person)

Workshops

Bars

Foundation, Level One

Creating Your Life

Right Voice For You

Right Relationship For You

Money Class

Rapid Results Workshop

<u>WORKSHOPS WITH NILOFER</u>

THE LATTICE EXPERIENCE

Enjoy 2 Extraordinary Days of Creation Where You Get To Co-Create Your Most Enlightened Life by Honoring Your Special Energy & Your Inner Uniqueness

<u>The Lattice Experience</u>

Evolutionary Foundations

This evolution of consciousness is accomplished by having a hands on experience of the first four phases of the EMF Balancing Technique®.

In Phases I-IV, you learn about the Universal Calibration Lattice. In Phase I your energy calibrates to balance your wisdom and your emotions. In Phase II your energy calibrates to integrate the wisdom of your history. In Phase III you focus upon your Core Energy and being present in now time. In Phase IV you gave conscious intent as you calibrate your potential.

<u>EMF Balancing Technique – Phases I – IV</u>

Master in Practice

In Phases V-VIII, you make conscious choices to practice the noble attributes of mastery in your daily life. Those choices create new energy patterns that continue to support you in your evolution.

As you experience these sessions and practice the attributes of mastery, the original resonance of who you are will increase. So will your ability to co-create the most enlightened life you can, filled with the noblest powers of Mastery!

"From the Infinite within me to the Infinite within you let us begin..."

~ Peggy Phoenix Dubro ~

Students describe the new sessions, and their experience in the Phases V-VIII classes:

"I experienced the original resonance of who I am present in every fiber of my being."

"The environment of love and trust, the feeling of family was a beautiful reso-nance; The step-up in the energy level was profound - the infinite possibilities of developing the 44 attributes of mastery (and more) are mind boggling."

"Phases V-VIII continues/deepens the foundations built in I-IV. Now I under-stand why we do the work the way we do - brilliant."

"Phases V-VIII sets templates within templates, creating a profound way to practice mastery...Each time a phase is offered it is unique, based on the cli-ent's choice of specific attributes, awesome!"

"Phases V-VIII begins another spiral that leads deep within, through ques-tions, the energy session, and the practice of mastery in daily life (with the help of 45 illustrated visuals presented in card form) The most profound work I have experienced."

EMF Balancing Technique – Phases V–VIII

Freedom! In The Energy of Love

In Phases IX-XII, you will further develop your ability to use the Third Lattice to manifest the energy of freedom within your being and your life. The dynamics of fission and fusion are used repeatedly to create a unique and powerful energy of evolution.

 I am astonished by the remarkable new energies now present in the work that we have been building together! Every phase of the EMF Balancing Technique assists you, as an individual, to joyfully evolve your under-standing and expression of wholeness.

In Phases IX-XII, you will gain a deeper understanding of your Core En-ergy as the ultimate expression of your self, your "Infinite I".

Here are some words from participants in the first Phases IX-XII train-ing:

*"**What a most beautiful opportunity to evolve** in a manner that is appropriate for each, as our Individual I (merges with) our Infinite I. These phases, nine to twelve, affect change in such a simple, quick, yet profound way. The phases have exceeded my grandest expectations of all that would take place! The energy of focusing on what we desire, the ideal, is so wonderfully in synchronicity with the new energies on the planet. How could we not evolve toward higher dimensions? Thank you Peggy, Stephen, and your family for bringing the EMF Balancing Technique to us in the fullness that now exists…"*

*"**So this is why we worked so hard** practicing Phases I-VIII all these years. Wow! This is what peace-filled empowerment means. What amazing tools for me as an Emerging Evolutionary! Thank you from deep in my heart Peggy and Stephen…"*

*"**This class was a stunning completion** to the EMF work and the promise of Phase XIII to come. I was more than satisfied! I am very excited about the future and our role in changing the consciousness of our world. Many of us have worked as much as 30 or more years for this "beginning moment"…"*

*"**Phases IX-XII are truly unique.** They are the next step or should I say leap in our evolution to wholeness. Those who make the commitment to receive these sessions are saying yes to all they can be…"*

*"**For me this has been in answer** to all my questions about everything I have read, heard or learned about the New Earth and the New Human working together one in one and empowering ourselves. First, doing all this work about my own process and then as I receive so much light, learning to give this incredible tool. Thanks to all this family for the work you have been doing…"*

EMF Balancing Technique – Phases IX – XII

The Way of the Evolutionary

Phase XIII, The Way of the Evolutionary, is a way to consciously direct your energy to create the life of your choice. The Lattice Logic understandings provide a lifestyle, a method of reasoning for you to experience what it means to think with your heart and feel with your mind as you direct your own energy.

"This session is a quick and direct way of touching a deep and profound space inside of yourself where you have greater clarity and focus. The Logic of the Lattice supports you in bringing out your inner wisdom during the session; And here is the best part – the support continues after the session! It goes with you because it IS you".

EMF Balancing Technique – Phase XIII

To contact Nilofer for further information about her books, audios, newsletters, workshops & training programs and consultancy or to schedule her for a presentation, please write to:

nilofer@illusiontoilluminationsummit.com

Websites are –
www.illusiontoilluminationsummit.com
www.healthylivingdubai.com
www.nilofersafdar.com
www.walkinginbalance.net

COPYRIGHT NOTICE

ACCESS CONSCIOUSNESS
COPYRIGHT NOTICE

Access Trademarks and Trade Names:

1. Access Consciousness®

2. Access Bars®

3. Conversations in Consciousness®

4. Energetic Synthesis of Being®

5. The Bars®

6. Right and Wrong, Good and Bad, POC, POD, all 9, shorts, boys and beyonds®

7. All of Life Comes To Me With Ease and Joy and Glory®

8. Ease, Joy and Glory®

9. How does it get any better than this?®

10. How does it get any better than that?®

11. The Body Whisperer®

12. What else is possible?®

13. Who does this belong to?®

14. Energetic Symphony of Being®

15. Energetic Synthesis of Being®

16. Symphony of Being®

17. Leaders for a Conscious World®

18. Consciousness Includes Everything and Judges Nothing®

19. Oneness Includes Everything and Judges Nothing®

*Scan this code to get free book updates, interviews, transcripts,
bonuses and great free training!*

SOME BONUS CONTENT :

1. Energy Exercises For Receiving Money

In this book I have shared several exercises for receiving money. Here are some of them-

Exercise - Using Your Limitations To Your Advantage

Buying Property

Exercise - Selling Property

Exercise - Contribution with Money

Exercise - What do you know about creating money

Exercise - What would you like to create your reality as?

Exercise - Receiving Beyond Barriers

Exercise - Creating Your Monetary Reality

Exercise - Moments of Magic with Money

2. Being Magical With Money

Nirmala Raju is also called Lottery Lady as she has won the lottery many times using her amazing clearing audios. She has created a phenomenal audio called Being Magical With Money. You actually get 2 here, one is in her voice (has a few technical glitches, ignore them) and one is in my voice. I wonder how much money will these bring?

3. Finally Having Money

In the last couple of months I have been using a clearing to create phenomenal possibilities with money. I have never shared this publicly before. I am gifting this clearing loop to you.

4. Clearing Loops From The Book

All the clearings from the book are recorded for you. You can play them as you eat, sleep, workout, drive or go for a walk. Create change without any of the hard work. Clearings that put you in the riding saddle of your money flows and allows a natural flow of abundant wealth.

THE ACCESS CONSCIOUSNESS CLEARING STATEMENT

The Clearing Statement is a tool you can use to change the energy of the points of view that have you locked into unchanging situations. You are the only one who can unlock the points of view that have you trapped. You will find the Clearing Statement throughout this book to unlock all the points of views about money that are keeping you stuck.

Clearing Statement: Right and Wrong, Good and Bad, POD, POC, All 9, Shorts, Boys and Beyonds®

Right and wrong, good and bad is shorthand for: What's right, good, perfect and correct about this? What's wrong, mean, vicious, terrible, bad, and awful about this? What have you decided is right and wrong, good and bad?

POD is the point of destruction immediately preceding whatever you decided.

POC is the point of creation of thoughts, feelings and emotions immediately preceding whatever you decided.

Sometimes instead of saying, "use the clearing statement," we just say, "POD and POC it."

All nine stands for nine layers of crap that we're taking out. You know that somewhere in those nine layers, there's got to be a pony because you couldn't put that much crap in one place without having a pony in there. It's crap you're generating yourself.

Shorts is the short version of: What's meaningful about this? What's meaningless about this? What's the punishment for this? What's the reward for this?

Boys stands for nucleated spheres. Have you ever seen one of those kid's bubble pipes? Blow here and you create a mass of bubbles? You pop one and it fills in, and you pop another one and it fills in. They're like that. You can never seem to get them all to pop.

Beyonds are feelings or sensations you get that stop your heart, stop your breath, or stop your willingness to look at possibilities. It's like when your business is in the red and you get another final notice and you go argh! You weren't expecting that right now. That's a beyond.

(The majority of information about the clearing statement is from the website www.theclearingstatement.com)

DATE DUE

AUG 0 6 2017	

BRODART, CO.   Cat. No. 23-221

CPSIA information can be obtained at www.ICGtesting.com
Printed in the USA
BVOW02s1815250416

445541BV00018B/167/P